you are
loved

you are loved

INSPIRING MESSAGES
FOR WOMEN

DESERET
BOOK

SALT LAKE CITY, UTAH

Interior art: andin/Adobe Stock
p. 114: supanut/Adobe Stock, Comauthor/Adobe Stock

Library of Congress Cataloging-in-Publication Data

CIP on file
ISBN 978-1-63993-259-7

Printed in China
RR Donnelley, Dongguan, China

10 9 8 7 6 5 4 3 2 1

CONTENTS

CONTENTS

We all have struggles.

Whether ours include something as small as frustration with an acquaintance or as big as grieving the death of a loved one, none of us have lives that look exactly how we might want them to. Sometimes, like Joseph Smith, we may feel the urge to cry, "O God, where art thou?" (Doctrine and Covenants 121:1).

In these moments of trial, how can we know we are loved? Not only by the people closest to us—though their love is essential too—but most of all, by the Creator of the Universe, our Father in Heaven? How do we come to not only believe but deeply *feel* the truth that "God is love" (1 John 4:16) and that He has "loved [us] with an everlasting love" (Jeremiah 31:3)?

In this collection of addresses by women for women, you will find messages exploring how we can recognize our divine worth and potential in times of both peace and trial. This book aims to help us know how we can feel the love of God and how we can share it, encouraging us to see ourselves and others the way God does—with grace, optimism, and love.

BE OF GOOD CHEER AND DO NOT FEAR

Irene Caso

Be of Good Cheer

When I think about being cheerful, I can't help but think about my maternal grandma, my abuela Isabel. She exemplifies to me what it is to be a cheerful person.

She didn't have an easy life. She lived through a civil war and a difficult marriage, miscarriages, economic difficulties, and health issues. But all I remember about her is her beautiful bright pink lips, her blue eye shadow, and her long and perfectly manicured nails. She had a beautiful smile and a very young spirit even at the age of ninety-three when she passed. She loved life and she lived it with passion.

When she was in her mid-thirties, her hip and one of her knees were severely damaged in a strange situation. What are the chances of a bank robbery in which the robbers take off in a high-speed chase that ends by crashing their getaway car against a streetlight and running over the only person walking on the street that early? Yes, my grandma was the person in the street. She never walked the same again and suffered a lot of pain throughout her life, but she always joked about it. When she came to visit, all the grandchildren would gather around her and fight to see who would help her take off her boots, then she would delight us with the amazing cracking noise that only her knee could make.

She never complained. I remember her sitting on a chair and dancing. She couldn't move her hips, but she sure could move and shake her shoulders to the beat of Frank Sinatra songs. Did my grandma speak or understand any English? No, not one word. But my grandma could sing "New York, New York," at the top of her lungs like she was the best of New Yorkers.

The invitation from the Lord to be of good cheer (like my grandma) is clear, and it's nothing new. There are many instances all throughout the scriptures when followers of Jesus Christ have been invited to be cheerful. Let me share a few.

To Nephi, the son of Nephi, who prayed for a full day because he was worried about the lives of those that believed in the prophecies of Samuel the Lamanite, the Lord answered and said, "Lift up your head and be of good cheer" (3 Nephi 1:13).

To the sick man with palsy, lying helpless on a bed, Jesus proclaimed, "Be of good cheer" (Matthew 9:2).

To the frightened Apostles fighting a violent sea, Jesus declared as He appeared on the water, "Be of good cheer" (Matthew 14:27).

As Joseph Smith met with ten elders about to be sent out, two by two, to missions that were potentially unsafe, the Lord announced, "Be of good cheer" (Doctrine and Covenants 61:36).

Speaking to the Apostles in His final moments before Gethsemane, Jesus said, "In the world ye shall have tribulation, but be of good cheer; I have overcome the world" (John 16:33).

In each of these scripture stories, the people had every reason to be anxious, fearful, and hopeless, yet the Lord directed them to rejoice.

So, here is the question: Why would the Lord be so persistent in teaching us to be cheerful? Why is this something repeated over and over again in the scriptures?

We're all taught as children to be happy by our parents, teachers, and those who surround us. We learn to sing songs about happiness: "If you are happy and you know it clap your hands,"[1] or are told to "turn that frown upside down." When I had some say in what clothes my kids would wear, I would look for clothes with smiley faces to help remind them that being happy is better than being sad. My thirteen-year-old boy, Diego, is tired of me telling him, "*Sonriendo te ves más guapo*" ("You look more handsome when you smile").

As a mother, my biggest desire for him and my daughter, Lola, is to be happy and to enjoy life. I'm sure I'm not the only one that desires that for her children.

I believe that our Heavenly Father and Savior have the same desires for us. They want us to be happy, and They are with us in the happiest times, but They also comfort us in the hardest moments of life. And in the same way I remind my son to smile, They remind us to be of good cheer—to lift our spirits up as we travel the often-difficult road of life.

I believe I'm not the only one to ask herself this question: Is it not enough that I have promised Heavenly Father that I will endure to the end and be longsuffering? Does He really still expect me to be happy along the way?

Yes, sisters, I believe so. The Lord tells us in the second half of Nephi 2:25, "Men are, that they might have joy." We're here on this earth to learn and make our way back to Heavenly Father, but also to have joy—to enjoy the process!

Think of your family or friends, the many gatherings and precious memories you have with them. Think of the good laughs you've experienced with other sisters, the first time you held a newborn baby, the sunrise, the sunset, the moonlight, online shopping, chocolate!

I could go on and on! Life is beautiful! It is not meant just to be endured. I believe making an effort to live with a positive outlook will protect us from the darts of the enemy and I believe that is one of the main reasons the Lord has asked us to be of good cheer.

When we are not making a conscious effort to stay positive, we don't remain neutral—we open the door to negative thoughts. One thing here, another one there, some resentment, some bitterness: it will all build up and drag us to a very negative and dark spot. It was little by little that the murmuring and complaining of Laman and Lemuel hardened their hearts, and little by little that the constant disobedience of Israel kept them wandering in the desert for forty years. We can each think of people who have been overcome by these negative emotions—including, sometimes, ourselves.

We can't expect to have a life free of trials. This life is a test, and at the end of day, the secret is "partaking of the bitter cup without becoming bitter."[2] This means accepting the will of the Lord even when it is not what we want or expected and keeping the faith to continue forward without resentment.

My parents are a great example to me, especially when it comes to going through the hardest of trials in life without being bitter.

They are considered "pioneers" of the Church in Spain, after joining the Church in 1977—the year religious freedom was declared after Spain had been under a dictatorship for decades.

Just four years before my parents met the missionaries, they had gone through the unimaginable pain of losing my older brother when he was two years old after he suffered a tragic accident at home.

As we can all imagine, losing Juan Carlitos devastated them. Their hearts were broken. They felt hopeless and empty. My mom would cry to my father, asking, "Why?" My father would hug her, shrug his shoulders, and answer, "I don't know, Isabel. I don't know, but one day we will get the answers."

They held strong to each other and their very basic faith in Christ. That, I believe, saved their marriage as they struggled through this tragedy.

An incredible thirst for knowledge overcame them. They felt something was missing. My mom remembers hoping she would find a place where she could dedicate herself to serving others. She specifically remembers wishing to be able to reach out to other women, wishing she had a place where they could support each other. She wondered if she should create an organization for women. Maybe write a book about her loss?

As a family, we believe it was no coincidence when Elder White and Elder Miller knocked on their apartment door. I know the Lord inspired these two wonderful missionaries to specifically ask my parents, in broken Spanish, if they could come in to share a message about Christ.

These words penetrated my parents' hearts. It didn't matter that they were about to have dinner or put the kids to bed; nothing mattered more to my parents than stopping whatever they were doing to hear these two missionaries teach them about the gospel of Jesus Christ. It was the additional knowledge and understanding they had desperately been seeking.

It turns out my mom didn't need to start an organization. It was already there for her. The beloved Relief Society was waiting for her. She was embraced by the other sisters and, over the years, she has been called by the Lord to serve and embrace other sisters. My parents have dedicated their lives to the Church and the work of the Lord.

The Lord's Church gave my parents the gospel and the tools they needed to overcome their difficult loss. Let me remind you that you and I are also blessed with the ability to overcome any trial or sadness of our heart because we know God's eternal plan.

Many years ago, during family home evening, one of my sisters surprised us with a drawing that she said represented our family. It was her way of expressing her love and the qualities she saw in each of us. I have always loved it. She chose to draw our family as a combination of flowers and plants. She carefully chose each one of these flowers and plants to match how she saw our personal attributes.

For example, framing the picture are my parents. My dad is the ivy because he is a quiet, hardworking man, someone that in a constant and steady way wraps around all of us and strengthens our home foundation. My mom is the reed, a strong plant that grows and nurtures itself by the living waters of a river. Like the reed that moves to follow the wind, my mom has always followed the Spirit, which has helped her guide our family. My oldest sister is a white rose because she is pure, innocent, and without guile. My brother is the blue flower and my other sister the poppy, and the little specs all over the painting represent my deceased brother, Juan Carlitos, who surrounds us like pollen, which we can all feel without seeing.

I was surprised to find that my sister saw me as a sunflower. She expressed how she admired my cheerful spirit and how I always looked on the bright side of life—not that I am always cheerful and positive, but I do try!

Sunflowers are amazing plants. They need six to eight hours of direct sunlight a day. Young sunflowers face east in the morning to greet the sun and turn from east to west over the course of each day, following the sun's light and brightness. Not only do they follow the light, but no matter how hard the winds are, they stand tall and continue looking at the sun!

Elder Quentin L. Cook said, "Like the young sunflower, when we follow the Savior of the world, the Son of God, we flourish and become glorious despite the many terrible circumstances that surround us. He truly is our light and life."[3]

If we create the habit in our lives of waking up every day, standing tall, and following the light like young sunflowers do, I guarantee that as we grow old and our testimonies mature, we will be like old sunflowers, which stop rotating. They stand firm and immovable, always looking east, constantly looking at the light.

Maybe in the biggest moments of our lives, we see a clear path to the Savior. But the real battle is won in the daily challenges of life. We have to decide each day to carry on, to keep going, to get out of bed despite all our unmet expectations, broken dreams, and the unrealized righteous desires of our heart. What do we do then? We offer our Heavenly Father the only gift we can offer Him: to stay faithful to Him, living the gospel the best we can.

We often ask ourselves, "Why am I not being blessed with this?" "When will I be blessed with that?" "Why are others blessed with it and not me?" "Why all this waiting?"

The miracle is to have all those questions wrapped up in the very core of your heart, but to still get ready to go to church, fulfil your calling, pick up the phone to minister to another sister, kneel to pray at night, and make it through the day with your best smile only to start all over again the next day.

My friend Sarai, who is like a sister to me, is a living example of this type of courage and faith. Sarai's mom, Mari Carmen, lost her husband, Luis, due to a tragic accident, leaving her with four young children who were three, six, nine, and twelve years old. Mari Carmen did an amazing job raising her children in the gospel of Jesus Christ despite the difficulties of being a widow. As Sarai was dating and looking for her future husband, she often told me she felt she could face any difficulty in life—but that she prayed she would never experience what her mom went through in being a widow. Sarai met a wonderful man named Sam, whom we all adored, and after under three years of marriage, he passed away from cancer at age thirty-five.

I could spend hours telling you about the beautiful ways Sarai has confronted this difficult loss and faced her worst fear while staying strong, with good cheer, serving others and serving the Lord. I don't know why these tragedies happen, but I can tell you that I have seen my friend rise, face her trials, and hold to the iron rod no matter what. She made that choice when Sam fought cancer, and to this day, holds to the iron rod.

Being of good cheer requires a conscious effort. We might not have control over the events in our lives, but we can control our reaction. Sister Marjorie Pay Hinckley said, "The only way to get through life is to laugh your way through it. You either have to laugh or cry. I prefer to laugh. Crying gives me a headache."[4]

I've often felt the same. Besides, science confirms the many benefits of laughter: it stimulates your heart, lungs, and muscles, and increases the endorphins that are released by your brain.

President Russell M. Nelson is also a great example to me of faith and optimism. He continues leading the Church through very difficult times, most recently through a pandemic that shocked the world and affected so many people. It robbed a lot of us of cheerfulness for a long time. As concern over COVID-19 continued and worship services were suspended worldwide, President Nelson posted a message of hope on his social channels, where he said in part, "These unique challenges will pass in due time. I remain optimistic for the future. I know the great and marvelous blessings that God has in store for those who love Him and serve Him."[5]

What a calming and reassuring promise from the Lord's prophet at a time when everything was so uncertain. I try to remember these words often. We are truly blessed to have a living prophet to remind us to be of good cheer even in the hardest times.

Do Not Fear

So now we know that we need to be of good cheer and that Heavenly Father has commanded us to try our best, but we all know that that isn't always the easiest thing to do. What is it that stops us from being cheerful?

It's fear: fear of not knowing for sure what the outcome will be, fear of not being enough, fear of change.[6]

I know about fear. Usually fear hits me the most in times of change. All the major changes in my life have come along with anxiety, self-doubt, and many, many tears (I'm very dramatic that way). I'll share a few examples.

I felt fear when my husband, Mike, asked me to marry him. As happy as I was and as excited as I was to start our life together, I returned to the apartment that I was sharing with my sister, ran to her, hugged her, and burst out in tears. She was so confused—she thought I had said no! She looked at Mike and asked him, "What did you do?!" I was crying because I was scared to leave my life with her behind, and because I knew that everything was about to change.

Several years later, I had another change in my life that brought fear. I had worked for twelve years as a news anchor and news director in a career I loved. I was comfortable and happy. Suddenly, the opportunity came for me to leave that behind and work as a media relations manager for the Church. I was filled with fear. Fear overcame me to the point that I asked for a priesthood blessing to calm my heart and to help me have the guidance I needed, which allowed me to follow what I can now see was the path the Lord wanted me to follow.

I'm sure that each of you could think of the many times throughout your life when you've had to face hard times or make difficult decisions, when you've faced fear and concerns about the unknown. Fortunately, we are blessed with the scriptures to find examples of those that faced fear in the most difficult circumstances.

Queen Esther teaches us a lot about being courageous in the face of fear. Esther could have backed down and stayed safe. Instead, she decided to stand up for her faith and her people. God called Esther to be brave, and I believe we have been extended the same invitation.

God equipped Esther for her battle when she decided to put her trust in Him before her own life. I believe the Lord does the same with us and will prepare us in the same way when we are facing fear and trials. He gave Esther the kind of faith and courage she needed to save the Jewish people from destruction and will give you the kind of faith you need to overcome whatever comes your way.

So how do we do it, then? How do we combat fear? Well, I can tell you what I do. Most of the time, fighting my fear involves attending the temple, praying, pondering, and calming my anxiety by walking our dog, Frida, while listening to general conference talks. Other times, I dance, sing, or listen to my favorite songs.

To lift our spirits and push through fear, my family has adopted a couple of sayings as themes for us that we remind each other of in difficult times.

First, I'm sure you've heard the saying "fake it till you make it." Our family uses this quite often, but with a twist. We don't say "fake it," since there's nothing fake about doing the things that we are supposed to do when our spirits are down or when grief is overpowering. I actually think that's heroic! What we say instead is "walk by faith until you know it." It's a reminder to keep going until brighter days come and to endure until the end because God gives you the strength to do so.

When I was growing up, my family and I loved playing the game Battleship. The object of Battleship is to sink the other player's ships before they sink yours. The other player's ships are somewhere on their board, and you can't see them. You try to hit them by calling out the coordinates of one of the squares on the board, and when you get lucky or have an educated guess and hit one of their ships, the other player has to announce if they've been "sunk" or "hit but not sunk." This is another phrase that we use sometimes to comfort one another as life throws its darts at us, as we experience loss, pain, loneliness, or dismay. We say to each other, "hit but not sunk," or "*tocada pero no hundida*," meaning that we might be hurt, but we're still here. Life is still beautiful, and we'll rise again.

Let me share one more thought about my grandma. There came a time in her life when she felt overwhelmed by difficulties. My grandpa was not religious and opposed her going to church, reading the Bible, or doing anything to do with faith.

However, my grandma was a very strong Christian and found a way to attend church services. On Sundays, she would tell the family that she was going to buy bread, and then secretly go to Mass. One day, her minister noticed how my grandma wasn't her cheerful self, and he talked with her. In a tearful reply, my grandma opened up to him. After that, her minister put his hands on her shoulders and told her, "Isabel, God made you *alegre*, cheerful; don't you let Him down." Those words changed my grandma's life and gave her the courage to go back to my grandpa, look him in the eyes, and let him know that yes, she got bread on Sundays, but that she had also been going to Mass and that from now on, she would be going every Sunday and that he was more than welcome to go with her.

I the Lord Am with You, and Will Stand by You

Now, I would like to focus on hope: the promise that we don't have to go through the difficulties and uncertainties of life alone and that the Lord is with us and will stand by us.

We find countless examples in the scriptures of those who have been afraid but have found the courage and the strength in the Lord to go through difficult circumstances and recognize His hand in the process: Nephi as he obeyed the Lord's command to return to Jerusalem to obtain the plates of brass, Noah as he built the ark to save his family, the pioneers as they crossed the plains to the Salt Lake Valley. None of them were ever alone, and the Lord was with them.

One of my favorite examples of this courage is Joshua. When Joshua was commanded by the Lord to lead the children of Israel into the land of promise without Moses, he was overwhelmed and afraid. Can you imagine? The great prophet Moses had led and guided Israel for over forty years, and now Joshua had that responsibility. A few years ago, when the bishop called me to serve as the Relief Society president, I could relate. I was young and inexperienced and scared to follow the most wonderful sister who had served so tirelessly and faithfully. I found strength in what the Lord told Joshua: "Have not I commanded thee? Be strong and of a good courage; be not afraid, neither be thou dismayed: for the Lord thy God is with thee whithersoever thou goest" (Joshua 1:9).

In the scripture, the Lord is extending this new calling to Joshua and He's trying to calm him down with reassuring words. Even with all that, though, the Lord also says, "Have not I commanded thee?" It reminds me of a parent repeating something to their kid for the millionth time! Let's look again at what we're being reminded: "Be not afraid, neither be thou dismayed: for the Lord thy God is with thee whithersoever thou goest." This is a beautiful promise that I know is extended to all of us.

We are never left alone. He is always there with a smile, His hand extended to us when we need it the most. I've felt the Lord's presence many times in my life, whether that's in the big things like losing dear friends and family members too early or when deciding to leave my home country to start a new life here in the United States, or the small things like being able to find a modest dress in a random mall in an international city while on a work assignment after the airline lost my luggage. Be of good cheer, don't fear, and trust that the Lord will be with you along the way.

Maybe you've heard the poem "The Race" by D. H. Groberg, which tells the story of a boy that starts a race hoping with all his heart to win because his father is watching and he wants to make him proud. Sadly, the boy falls again and again, getting more and more behind. Each time he feels discouraged, knowing that with each fall he has lost any chance of winning and that his dad, watching from a distance, is probably disappointed. But each time he falls, he gets back up and runs as hard as he can because he can hear the voice of his dad: "You haven't lost at all. For winning is no more than this: to rise each time you fall." As you can predict, the boy finishes the race in last place, but the crowd cheers as loudly for him as for the winner.

The last verse of the poem reads:

> *And now when things seem dark and bleak*
> *And difficult to face,*
> *The memory of that little boy*
> *Helps me in my own race.*
>
> *For all of life is like that race,*
> *With ups and downs and all.*
> *And all you have to do to win,*
> *Is rise each time you fall.*
>
> *And when depression and despair*
> *shout loudly in my face,*
> *another voice within me says,*
> *"Get up and win that race!"* [7]

Like the boy in that poem, we need to win the race of this mortal life by coming back to the loving arms of our Heavenly Father, who has been there all along the way, cheering for us as we have fallen over and over.

Stay firm, put up the good fight, and stay strong in the

gospel, holding to the iron rod and not letting go. Don't add unnecessary bumps to your race—unnecessary heartaches that are consequences of sin—and when you fall, be quick to repent, wipe off your knees, and come back to the race. I pray that you are able to do so cheerfully, singing and dancing all the way to the end. You can do it; you *are* doing it! Just keep going. We are all here to lift each other up.

Heavenly Father loves you and He hears you. You are not alone. Jesus Christ has felt your sorrows, and He knows them. Not a single ache of your heart goes unnoticed.

NOTES

1. *Children's Songbook*, "If You're Happy," 266.
2. Neal A. Maxwell, "Apply the Atoning Blood of Christ," *Ensign*, November 1997.
3. Quentin L. Cook, "The Lord Is My Light," *Liahona*, May 2015.
4. Pearce, ed. *Glimpses into the Life and Heart of Marjorie Pay Hinckley* (1999), 107.
5. Russell M. Nelson, "Today I shared an important message about a remedy for our current situation: the healing power of gratitude. I invite you to watch this video and follow the invitations given. #GiveThanks," Twitter, November 20, 2020, 11:04 am, https://twitter.com/Nelson RussellM/status/1329848023363383297.
6. See Doctrine and Covenants 68:6.
7. Dee Groberg, *The Race: Life's Greatest Lesson*, Faithwords, 2004.

LIGHT IN UNEXPECTED PLACES

Michelle D. Craig

On the way to the recycling bin, as I was thumbing through a magazine that had come in the mail, I saw a page that stopped me in my tracks. It was an image of a painting by Caitlin Connolly entitled "Holding Holy Things."

In this painting, a woman carries a collection of plain white stones. Her face is weary, but she is surrounded by color and light, and the stones in her hands glow with the power of the Lord.

I tore the page out of the magazine and, through tear-filled eyes, thought about how often I feel like the woman depicted in the painting—bringing my meager offerings, my rocks, to the Lord and asking for miracles, asking for His light and His hand in my life. My offerings have become "holy things" as I have climbed high mountains and have sought to have my rough places made smooth, "notwithstanding my weakness" (2 Nephi 33:11).

At times all of us feel overwhelmed with the demands of our circumstances:

- Too many children—or not enough.
- A calling that demands more time and energy than we have—or perhaps a feeling of being underutilized.
- Bodies, minds, and relationships that need healing.
- Financial stress that feels weighty.

The list could go on and on—you know; you have your own list. Yet we get out of bed every day and want to bring the Lord our very best, ordinary offerings. You bring your sixteen small stones—and you ask for miracles.

I would like to share some principles from this story and others found in scripture about small stones, light, faith in Jesus Christ, grace, and miracles—principles that help give me perspective when I find myself coming up short again and again and again!

There Is a Difference between Weakness and Sin.

Many of us are familiar with the scripture found in Ether 12:27: "And if men come unto me I will show unto them their weakness. I give unto men weakness that they may be humble."

Weakness in this verse is singular, not plural. Weakness is a condition of mortality; it can help us experience how very much we need the Lord.

Elder Richard G. Scott taught that "the Lord sees weaknesses differently than He does rebellion. Whereas the Lord warns that unrepented rebellion will bring punishment, when the Lord speaks of weaknesses, it is always with mercy."[1]

We should never question that in His mercy, the Lord is ready, willing, and anxious to help us overcome our weaknesses.

Recognizing Weakness Is a Catalyst to Change

In Ether 12:37, the Lord says to Moroni, "Because thou hast seen thy weakness thou shalt be made strong." He is not offering to change Moroni's weakness, but to change *Moroni*, because Moroni recognized his weakness and shortcomings. Those who do not see weakness simply do not progress. This awareness is a blessing; it keeps us humble and turning to the Savior.

It was after Peter had been invited to "launch out into the deep" and "let down [his] nets" (Luke 5:4) after a long night of fishing and nothing to show for it that the miracle occurred—so many fish that the boats began to sink.

Peter fell at the feet of Jesus and cried out, "I am a sinful man, O Lord" (Luke 5:8). He certainly recognized and acknowledged weakness in this moment. His words and subsequent actions show us that as we get closer to Jesus Christ, we become aware of our weakness and we desire His help in becoming more like Him.

President Ezra Taft Benson taught, "Men and women who turn their lives over to God will discover that He can make a lot more out of their lives than they can."[2] This is what happened to Peter and the other disciples. Jesus helped them realize they could do more than catch fish—they could become, with His help, "fishers of men" (Matthew 4:19).

As we recognize our weakness, desire to change, and rely on Jesus Christ, our very natures can change. We too can experience the promise found in 2 Nephi 3:13: "Out of weakness [we] shall be made strong."

Discontent Can Be Divine

Calls to action from prophets, seers, and revelators or from the Holy Ghost, along with our innate sense that we can do and be more, sometimes create within us what Elder Neal A. Maxwell called "divine discontent." Divine discontent comes when we compare what we are to what we have the power to become. Each of us, if we are honest, feels this gap. We yearn for greater personal capacity; we want to do more and be more. We have these feelings because we are daughters and sons of God, born with the Light of Christ, yet we live in a fallen world. These feelings can be a blessing because they can propel us to action and greater discipleship.

Satan knows this as well and would have us see our weakness as a sign of failure. He would have us wallow in despair and discouragement, focusing on all that we are not—lacking in capacity, looks, finances, personality, health, talent, you name it. We all come up short in something. Our discontent can become destructive when we listen to and believe the messages Satan bombards us with, or it can become divine when we turn to Jesus Christ with humility.

One of my earliest memories is coming face-to-face with my shortcomings. I remember starting kindergarten with the goal to never make a mistake—ever. I remember getting the very first worksheet—my first chance to do something perfectly. There were two columns of pictures and we were to match Goldilocks on one side of the paper to the three bears on the other. I took my time but wasn't quite sure I had done it right. At recess in the kindergarten courtyard, some of us compared notes, and to my horror, I realized I had done something wrong. My very first worksheet on my very first day, and I had already made a mistake. So I ran and hid. I stayed in my hiding spot when the bell rang, and everyone went inside. It wasn't long before the teacher came looking and assured me that all was not lost. I was going to be okay.

Fast forward a few years to my baptism day. I had a goal. You've got it—I was going to be perfect. Well, I was pretty good for an hour or two. I can't remember exactly what happened, but I do remember being outside with a lot of family and getting mad at one of my brothers. I probably said something unkind. I don't remember the words, but I do remember the sinking feeling that came as I realized I had sinned. It had only been a few hours, and I had already blown it. So what did I do? Yes, I ran and hid. But this time, no one came looking. After some time, I realized I must eventually come out of my hiding place. The message to *run and hide* comes directly from Satan's playbook. We see this pattern in scripture and in the temple (see Moses 4:14). We are taught the Lord's solution to mistakes and sin in those very same places. Faith is a principle of action; the Lord loves effort.

Back to the account of the brother of Jared: he had a problem, and he took that problem to the Lord. The barges he had built to cross the ocean had no light. "Behold, O Lord, wilt thou suffer that we shall cross this great water in darkness?" (Ether 2:22). After crying unto the Lord in prayer, the brother of Jared did not go home and wait for an angel to deliver the solution—he went to work. As disciples of Jesus Christ, we must remember that "it is not meet that [the Lord] should command in all things"

(Doctrine and Covenants 58:26). Like the brother of Jared, we must carefully evaluate those things in our lives that we need to start doing, stop doing, and continue doing. There will not be a "one size fits all" answer to most of our needs. The same words of the Lord given to the brother of Jared as he was instructed to build those barges—"go to work and build"—apply to each of us (Ether 2:16). We aren't in the business of building barges, but we are in the business of building up people and building up testimonies as we invite others to come unto Christ. Take your plans to the Lord in prayer. This will require faith and effort on your part. Living as a disciple of Jesus Christ requires work. As He did with the stone offerings of the brother of Jared, the Lord will touch your efforts as you seek His assistance. The brother of Jared showed us how faith is exercised by moving our feet. President Harold B. Lee taught: "If you want the blessing, don't just kneel down and pray about it. Prepare yourselves in every conceivable way you can in order to make yourselves worthy to receive the blessing you seek."[3]

The brother of Jared climbed up a mountain, a mountain of "exceeding height," to find some stones. He didn't take the first rocks he found, but rather he did "molten out of a rock sixteen small stones; and they were white and clear, even as transparent glass" (Ether 3:1). He did everything he could do on his own, and then he took it to the Lord. To turn the rock into smooth, clear stones, he had to subject it to great heat—a refining process that could be compared to life. As we trust God, strive to live the commandments, make and keep sacred covenants, and serve others, the rough edges become smoothed. We become like the stones presented to the Lord by the brother of Jared—stones that were ordinary, meager offerings that were set aflame with enduring light when touched—one by one—by the Lord.

I love the account of Enoch in latter-day scripture. Enoch had received a call from the Lord that overwhelmed him. "Why is it that I have found favor in thy sight, and am but a lad, and all the people hate me; for I am slow of speech; wherefore am I thy servant?" (Moses 6:31). The Lord's advice: "Open thy mouth, and it shall be filled, and I will give thee utterance" (Moses 6:32).

How many of us feel similar to Enoch at times? We are called by the Lord to do something that is hard. Sometimes that difficulty is because we live in a fallen world. We feel that what is being asked of us is beyond our abilities and capacity. Perhaps we want to run and hide. More than once I have cried out to the Lord with my lack. How can my rocks, my five loaves and fishes, possibly be enough for what is being asked of me? All of us come up short. We simply don't have enough time, patience, energy, brain power, or capacity.

We do not see any suggestion that Enoch doubted the promise given by the Lord. He simply went to work with obedience and faith.[4] President Thomas S. Monson taught, "Remember that this work is not yours and mine alone. It is the Lord's work, and when we are on the Lord's errand, we are entitled to the Lord's help. Remember that whom the Lord calls, the Lord qualifies."[5]

Power to Convert a Weakness to a Strength Is Possible through the Grace of Jesus Christ

Enoch's story reveals the amazing power of God's grace—power that each one of us can experience to some degree as we move forward with faith in Him. "As Enoch spake forth the words of God, the people trembled, and could not stand in his presence" (Moses 6:47).

In fact, "so great was the faith of Enoch that . . . he spake the word of the Lord, and the earth trembled, and the mountains fled, even according to his command; and the rivers of water were turned out of their course; . . . and all nations feared greatly, so powerful was the word of Enoch, and so great was the power of the language which God had given him" (Moses 7:13).

All this from a "lad" who was "slow of speech" (Moses 6:31). The grace of Jesus Christ transforms and protects.

I bear testimony that the verse found in Philippians 4:13 is true: "I can do all things through Christ which strengtheneth me." The power to convert a weakness to a strength, to accomplish those things we are asked to do, is possible through the grace of Jesus Christ.[6]

Miracles Can Come from Our Meager Offerings

The story of sixteen small stones teaches us that our Savior can do anything and can bring His light into the most unexpected places in the most unexpected ways. He can do extraordinary things with a rock! So, on those days when you feel ordinary, when you feel like your best maybe isn't good enough, remember that God isn't asking any of us to be perfect before blessing us for our imperfect efforts. What He requires from us is our hearts and a willing mind.[7] What He is asking from us is that we do all that we can—we offer our loaves and small fishes, our rocks—and we give them willingly to Jesus Christ. He magnifies and touches our offerings and they become enough—and to spare.

Elder Lawrence E. Corbridge taught, "For those of us who feel wanting when it comes to talents and gifts, it is encouraging to know that [the Savior's invitation to 'let your light so shine before men'] is not to dazzle others with who *we* are or what *we* know. Rather, our light is the Light of the World [our Savior, Jesus Christ,] reflected in us as we simply strive to do as He did. That's it. The Lord tells us to follow Him and not be ashamed or unwilling to stand out. Do not be ashamed to hold up His light. Do not be afraid to shine. Do not worry about the outcome."[8]

President James E. Faust shared this bit of wisdom: "Occasionally . . . you are too hard on yourselves. You think that if your offering is not quite perfect, it is not acceptable. I tell you, however, that if you have done your best, which you usually do, your humble offering, whatever it may be, will be acceptable and pleasing to the Lord."[9]

A Witness Comes after the Trial of Our Faith

The brother of Jared faced a trial of faith, and the witness he received was twofold. The desired blessing came: the stones were touched, and they were filled with light. But even more important was what happened in the process. As the Lord touched the stones, the brother of Jared saw the finger of the Lord. Because of his great faith, the Lord showed Himself to the brother of Jared, saying, "Behold, I am he who was prepared from the foundation of the world to redeem my people. Behold, I am Jesus Christ" (Ether 3:14).

When we trust God and allow Him to prevail in our lives, the end result will be better than we could possibly imagine. When the brother of Jared climbed the mountain and presented his best effort, sixteen stones, he probably was not expecting to see Jesus Christ. But he did.

Notwithstanding our weakness, like the brother of Jared, the most important miracle we can experience is a knowledge that Jesus Christ lives—that His light can shine in our lives and in the lives of those we serve.

NOTES

1. Richard G. Scott, "Personal Strength through the Atonement of Jesus Christ," *Ensign* or *Liahona*, November 2013.
2. Ezra Taft Benson, "Jesus Christ—Gifts and Expectations," *Ensign*, December 1988.
3. Harold B. Lee, *Stand Ye in Holy Places* [1974], 243–44.
4. See Moses 6:42.
5. Thomas S. Monson, "Duty Calls," *Ensign*, May 1996.
6. See 2 Corinthians 12:9.
7. See Doctrine and Covenants 64:34.
8. Lawrence E. Corbridge, "Valiant in the Testimony of Jesus Christ," *Ensign*, September 2011.
9. James E. Faust, "Instruments in the Hands of God, *Ensign* or *Liahona*, November 2005.

GOD'S LOVE: THE MOST JOYOUS TO THE SOUL

Sunny Mahe

My testimony begins with a knowledge of God's love that echoes Nephi's: "I know that he loveth his children; nevertheless, I do not know the meaning of all things" (1 Nephi 11:17).

In reference to God's love, President Thomas S. Monson said, "It is simply always there."[1]

But I also know that in my life that there have been times that it has been difficult to feel that love. I want to expose a few of the obstacles I have experienced that make it difficult to feel God's love and present some practical ways to make feeling it easier.

So, why is it sometimes difficult to feel God's love? The three obstacles I want to focus on are:

1. We experience trials.
2. We do not recognize answers to prayers.
3. We do not feel worthy or enough.

We Experience Trials

In 2016, my husband and I had eight children, including our three-year-old daughter, Elsie. Elsie was full of life and mischief. She picked neighbors' flowers and made herself peanut butter hats. She was playful and silly. She was terribly afraid of BYU's Cosmo the Cougar.

On Tuesday, November 22, 2016, I was at home with the three littlest ones after sending the big kids off to school. I had a neighbor's two kids over to play with Elsie and Tank. I was busy with household chores and the kids were alternately laughing, playing nicely together, and then tattling about saying sassy words or not sharing toys.

At one point, as I was washing the dishes in the kitchen, Elsie's little friend tapped me on the hip and said, "Elsie's hanging by the string." That seemed like a strange thing to tattle about, and I didn't think much of it until she followed up with, "No, like she needs help."

I was a little frustrated as I thought of how I never got anything done around the house. So, I didn't even turn off the water in the sink before walking to the front room, where I found Elsie had become entangled in a cord from our window blinds.

I quickly took her down and began CPR, even starting her heart and getting her to take breaths on her own before the paramedics came. But even though we experienced many miracles that gave us great hope, ultimately, my funny, naughty, full-of-life Elsie died after a week in the hospital.

I guess a part of me thought that when you are doing the

good things and checking the boxes, you could expect a certain amount of protection from these kinds of trials. I mean—I was doing service, right? I was washing dishes for my family and watching a friend's kids so she could go to an appointment. Isn't that how it works? We do all we can, and God makes up the rest by protecting us from heartache.

Elder D. Todd Christofferson said, "We ought not to think of God's plan as a cosmic vending machine where we (1) select a desired blessing, (2) insert the required sum of good works, and (3) the order is promptly delivered."[2]

He goes on to explain that while our obedience and good works matter, it is more because of the way those things change us and make us better rather than because we are purchasing blessings or protection.

I hate to be the bearer of bad news, but I can testify today that the cosmic vending machine is broken. So if that's not how it works, then how do we protect ourselves from painful trials?

Well, more bad news: we don't.

All of us must experience trials here on this earth. And our trials will be big; they will be heavy and difficult. It can seem like a loving Father would not subject His children to such burdens. But there are countless examples in the scriptures that teach us that no matter how righteous you are, you will have trials. Having trials, even big, painful ones, is not an accurate measuring stick of whether we are loved by God.

There seems to be no limit to the number of ways that a heart can break—whether it be through our own choices, the choices of others that affect us, or the natural consequences of living in a fallen world. But we came here to become like Christ, and that requires difficulty.

Elder Neal A. Maxwell said, "Therefore, how can you and I really expect to glide naively through life, as if to say, 'Lord, give me experience, but not grief, not sorrow, not pain, not opposition, not betrayal, and certainly not to be forsaken. Keep from me, Lord, all those experiences which made Thee what Thou art! Then let me come and dwell with Thee and fully share Thy joy!'"[3]

You are loved through your trials, but you will have them. If you find yourself currently in a season of relative ease, take the time to gather strength and oil for your testimony lamp because trials are not an opt-in part of this earthly experience.

We Do Not Recognize Answers
to Prayers (The Drowning Man)

A man was stuck on his rooftop in a flood, so he prayed to God for help.

Soon, a man in a rowboat came by and the fellow shouted to the man on the roof, "Jump in, I can save you."

The stranded man shouted back, "No, it's okay. I'm praying to God, and he is going to save me."

So, the rowboat went on.

Then a motorboat came by. The woman in the motorboat shouted, "Jump in, I can save you."

To this the stranded man said, "No thanks, I'm praying to God, and he is going to save me. I have faith."

So, the motorboat went on.

Then a helicopter came by, and the pilot shouted down, "Grab this rope and I will lift you to safety."

To this the stranded man again replied, "No thanks, I'm praying to God, and he is going to save me. I have faith."

So, the helicopter reluctantly flew away.

Soon the water rose above the rooftop and the man drowned. He went to heaven. He finally got his chance to discuss this whole situation with God, at which point he exclaimed, "I had faith in you, but you didn't save me. You let me drown. I don't understand why!"

To this God replied, "I sent you a rowboat and a motorboat and a helicopter, what more did you expect?"

This story illustrates a point Spencer W. Kimball also made when he said, "God does notice us, and he watches over us. But it is usually through another person that he meets our needs."[4]

Sometimes the answers to our prayers don't look the way we think they should.

In 2 Kings 4, the widow of a faithful disciple approaches the prophet Elisha to tell him that her deceased husband left her in terrible debt and that her creditors are coming to collect her sons to be slaves.

He says, "Well, what do you have?"

She answers, "Nothing. I mean, I guess I have that small pot of oil."

He tells her to gather up all of her neighbors' extra pots and dump her oil in there.

Surely this was not the response she was expecting: "Dump

out even the last thing you have." But God works in unexpected ways sometimes. Her oil multiplied enough to fill all of the pots that she had, so much so that she sold the excess and was able to pay off the debt that she owed as well as provide an income for her family moving forward.

Elder Richard G. Scott said, "Find the compensatory blessings in your life when, in the wisdom of the Lord, He deprives you of something you very much want. To the sightless or hearing impaired, He sharpens the other senses. . . . With the loss of a dear one, He deepens the bonds of love, enriches memories, and kindles hope in a future reunion."[5]

I know very well the temptation to reject the compensatory blessings that God sends. In the case of the widow who received oil to provide for her family, I have to believe that she would have preferred to have her husband restored to her.

When I was in the hospital with Elsie, I wondered how I could ever feel safe in my home again. Our home had always been a sanctuary of joy and love and safety, but it now held the memories of the worst moments of my whole life.

So when my wonderful neighbors, friends, and even strangers took that week we were in the hospital to remodel, repair, and replace things in our home so that we would feel loved, I had the temptation to say, "Actually, what I really want is my Elsie."

How silly it would have been for me to reject the overwhelming compensatory blessings bestowed upon me through the kindness of all those people that turned my home into a temple of service and love.

It would have also been easy to say, "My prayers for healing weren't answered. So God doesn't answer my prayers."

But actually, sometimes the answer is no.

Occasionally, one of my children will ask me for a snack because they say they are hungry. But what they mean is, "I saw the hidden stash of Oreos and I want them." When I offer them a banana or an apple as a solution to their hunger, it can seem to them like maybe that's not a great solution. They might even say that I am mean or selfish or unloving.

Sometimes we might feel the same way about God when our prayers are answered differently than the way we hope.

But we read in Matthew 7:9–11, "Or what man is there of you, whom if his son ask bread, will he give him a stone? Or if he ask a fish, will he give him a serpent? If ye then, being evil, know how to give good gifts unto your children, how much more shall your Father which is in heaven give good things to them that ask him?"

When we have prayed for the miracle of healing and we receive instead the miracle of peace and comfort, we can feel much like my Oreo-deprived children. Perhaps you find yourself feeling similarly about the Lord's version of an answer to your prayers that looks different from how you would have liked Him to answer. To you I would say, "Give the banana a try. It may be just what you didn't know you needed."

Since Elsie's passing, I can report that trials are still an active part of our lives. Some of my most painful battles have been fought since Elsie died—many of them too personal to share publicly. But I believe that someday I will look back and feel truly grateful that I had someone so invested in our family's success helping us from the other side of the veil.

We Do Not Feel Worthy or Enough

This brings us to the next obstacle: feeling God's love.

With her permission, I share this story of a dear friend who owns a calligraphy print business. She creates beautiful prints of meaningful quotes and uplifting messages. Recently, I asked her to create a set of prints for an Easter event I was hosting. I gave her a vague explanation of what I was hoping for, but really, I wasn't even sure what I wanted. I told her I wanted a set of three simple prints that would say *Gethsemane*, *Golgotha*, and *Garden Tomb*. I know several graphic designers, but I specifically chose this friend because she had been battling cancer and I wanted to support her business.

Well, my friend took time studying and praying about this assignment. She sent me the first draft of what she had come up with, along with lengthy descriptions of the symbolism behind each pen stroke and color choice. They were beautiful—but not quite was I was looking for.

I gave a few more vague instructions, and she went back to designing.

Finally, she sent me a simple graphic that said each of the words in a basic, almost childlike font. Each of the prints had a simple graphic above the word—an olive branch, a cross on a hill, and an open tomb.

When I saw her art, my heart leapt and I said, "Yes! This is exactly what I was hoping for! I LOVE IT!"

It wasn't until later that she told me the miracle of this experience.

You see, what I didn't know was that my friend had been so weak and sick that she could barely hold a pen. She had been embarrassed to send me what she had come up with. The rudimentary lines and rustic look of the font represented the best that she was capable of doing at the time. The fact that it was exactly what I wanted became a testimony to her that our best is not only good enough, but it is exactly what the Lord wants—even when it doesn't seem good enough to us.

Sometimes, we do not feel the Lord's love because we have fallen away from the covenant path, in which case the answer is to repent and return. But often we do not feel worthy of the Lord's love simply because of our own insecurities about our inadequacies and weaknesses, combined with whisperings from the adversary that we can never measure up.

I often still struggle with this. Since Elsie died, I have battled voices in my head that tell me that I have failed society's lowest standard for mothers: just keep the kids alive. When my home gets messy, I think about those dishes in the sink the day of Elsie's accident and hear voices that say, "If you had kept your house cleaner, Elsie wouldn't have had that accident."

When my children get injured or sick, those voices say, "You can't keep them safe."

When I gain weight those voices say, "See? You can't even take care of yourself. Why would you be able to take care of anyone else?"

But there always seems to be another voice that whispers, "You are enough because you are Mine."

The parable of the shepherd that leaves the ninety-nine sheep to find the one that was lost always seemed like a bummer to me. As a general rule, I like to find myself in the middle of the flock. I'm a rule follower by nature and I have never been very rebellious. So, I always felt like maybe I didn't matter that much if I was one of the ninety-nine. And then I found myself as the one.

I now had a problem that was absolutely unfixable. My daughter was gone, and I could not bring her back. I felt lost and alone, ashamed and afraid. And it was in this place that I discovered the power of His love for the one. Eventually, at some point, we are all the one.

Recently, I learned more about God's love for the one. My daughter Ellie missed her midnight curfew and had let her phone die. I was left pacing on the floor, unsure where she was and unable to reach her. 12:00 became 12:15, became 12:30, became 12:45, became 1:00.

Was she okay? Was she stuck somewhere she shouldn't be and in a compromising situation? Was she in an accident? Was she in the hospital? Was she going to fall asleep at the wheel on the drive home? I was spiraling into panic more and more with each passing minute.

I had a feeling I knew where she might be. So finally, at 1:30 am, I woke up another child to sleep near the baby and I ran to my car to find my little lost sheep.

I finally understood the scripture Luke 15:4–6: "What man

of you, having an hundred sheep, if he lose one of them, doth not leave the ninety and nine in the wilderness, and go after that which is lost, until he find it? And when he hath found it, he layeth it on his shoulders, rejoicing. And when he cometh home, he calleth together his friends and neighbours, saying unto them, Rejoice with me; for I have found my sheep which was lost."

Whether you are the one or part of the ninety-nine, no one is dispensable. My daughter Ellie is irreplaceable. So am I. So are you. Even when you do not feel worthy of it or when you feel like you are not enough, God loves you. He knows your name. And He asks you to take His.

So how can we remember God's love and successfully move past the obstacles that keep us from feeling it?

My three best tools are:

1. Scripture study.
2. Cleaving to covenants.
3. Gratitude.

Scripture Study

Elder Robert D. Hales said, "When we want to speak to God, we pray. And when we want Him to speak to us, we search the scriptures."[6]

One of my favorite personal examples of a prayer being answered through scripture was in 2008, when we had just moved back to Utah.

I grew up in Texas. My husband, Reno, however, went to high

school in Utah. He was a high school football standout, and then he played at BYU. After we got married and moved back east so he could play for the Philadelphia Eagles, occasionally he would be recognized, but most often we enjoyed a little bit of anonymity.

When we eventually moved back to Utah, a well-meaning bishop sought me out immediately after sacrament meeting the first Sunday we attended that ward, asking for Reno, who had stepped out into the hallway.

He said, "Sister Mahe! We have the best calling for your husband!" And then, seeing I was somewhat unimpressed by that, he followed up with, "Don't worry. We'll find somewhere to stick you later."

While it is a little embarrassing to admit, the pin to the balloon of my overinflated ego was a bit painful for me. I felt silly and small. I felt unimportant and forgotten. I thought, "I used to be somebody! I trained for the Olympics! Is this just who I am forever now? Reno Mahe's wife?" (You'll be happy to know that I've since then embraced the title).

At the time, though, it bothered me enough that I took it to prayer. When I opened my scriptures, I turned to 1 Nephi 21:15–16, which says, "For can a woman forget her sucking child, that she should not have compassion on the son of her womb? Yea, they may forget, yet will I not forget thee, O house of Israel. Behold, I have graven thee upon the palms of my hands; thy walls are continually before me."

Yes, people will forget us. They may disappoint us or hurt us. But God will never forget us.

I know that we can feel God's love for us through the scriptures. He sends us love notes every day. Will we read them?

Cleave to Covenants

I was blessed with a super surprise bonus baby who we recently noticed was flexing her stomach as if she wanted to sit up, so we started doing little ab workouts with her. She holds onto our fingers, and we gently lift her up and slowly roll her back down on her back, making sure she doesn't fall. She is gaining strength, but it is likely really difficult for her. Still, who is actually doing most of the work?

I was reminded of this scripture, Matthew 11:29–30: "Take my yoke upon you, and learn of me; for I am meek and lowly in heart: and ye shall find rest unto your souls. For my yoke is easy, and my burden is light."

We yoke ourselves to the Savior by making covenants and cleaving to them as we do the things He asks us to do. This is what makes His burden light. He lets us carry enough to gain strength, which feels very difficult for us sometimes. He allows us to take part in the work of salvation, but the reality is that He is actually the one doing all the work. For me, cleaving to my covenants means holding my Savior's hands.

Gratitude

My best tool for feeling God's love is gratitude. This might seem counterintuitive, but I have come to notice that *even our trials come from our blessings.*

Reno retired from playing professional football in 2008. We quickly bought a beautiful home near market peak right before the housing market crashed. Within weeks, we lost every dollar we had invested and found ourselves upside down in our new home. We lived for about a year on savings, about a year on credit, and somehow continued scraping by as Reno learned about business and became an entrepreneur. It was a steep learning curve. Amidst the financial struggles, we were also unknowingly involved in a close friend's illegal activities and Reno was very publicly charged with a crime he did not commit. It was a season of loss—loss of income, loss of reputation and friendships, loss of our family Suburban. Still, each of those losses can be attributed to previous blessings.

We lost all of our money . . . but Reno played in the NFL! We had money to lose!

We lost our good name and reputation . . . but enough people knew about us to care!

A few years later, when we lost our daughter . . . well, we have a daughter! So many yearn for that blessing.

When we focus on gratitude for the blessings we have received and notice the compensatory blessings for the ones we feel we have been denied, we push away bitterness and are able to feel joy in spite of our sorrows. There is nothing that we can teach the Savior about suffering or unfairness. He may take our financial security. He may take our reputation. He may take our family car. He may take our beloved family members.

But in return, if we are faithful, we are promised all that the Father has. In return, He raises our daughters from the dead.

Sisters, it is my hope that you will be filled with God's love for you. I hope that you will discover all of the creative ways that He finds to show His love to you, and that you will remember the lyrics to a well-known hymn.

God loved us, so He sent His Son
Christ Jesus, the atoning One
To show us by the path He trod
The one and only way to God.

Oh, love effulgent, love divine!
What debt of gratitude is mine,
That in his off'ring I have part
And hold a place within his heart.[7]

We hold a place within His heart.

NOTES

1. Thomas S. Monson, "We Never Walk Alone," *Ensign* or *Liahona*, November 2013.
2. D. Todd Christofferson, "Our Relationship with God," *Liahona*, May 2022.
3. Neal A. Maxwell, "Lest Ye Be Wearied and Faint in Your Minds," *Ensign*, May 1991.
4. *Teachings of Presidents of the Church: Spencer W. Kimball* (2006), 82.
5. Richard G. Scott, "Finding Joy in Life," *Ensign*, May 1996.
6. Robert D. Hales, "Holy Scriptures: The Power of God unto Our Salvation," *Ensign* or *Liahona*, November 2006.
7. "God Loved Us, So He Sent His Son," *Hymns*, no. 187.

REMOVING THE FEELING OF FOREVER FALLING SHORT

Rebecca L. Craven

I am painfully aware of my weakness and my weaknesses. And I'm certain I have many more that I'm just not willing to ask Heavenly Father to show me right now. What I love about our Father in Heaven is that He is not fixated on our weakness or what we can or cannot do. He is focused on our progress! He is focused on *us*!

It's important to understand that weakness and sin are not the same thing. Sin is willfully disobeying God's commandments or failing to act righteously despite knowing truth.[1] Sin is a choice that leads us away from God.

Weakness, in contrast, is a "condition of being mortal."[2] It's the lack of ability, strength, or skill and is part of each of us in unique and individual ways. Remember, we came to earth knowing absolutely *nothing!* But isn't it wonderful that we are here? Just think of all you have learned! We wanted this mortal experience where we could acquire knowledge and learn how to make good choices and grow to become like our heavenly parents.

Unlike sin, weakness can bring us *closer* to God. We learn in Ether 12 that the Lord gave us weakness in the hope that we would become humble and teachable enough for Him to transform our weak places into strongholds. This growth comes line upon line until we someday reach perfection. But it will not happen in this life! *So, breathe!*

Elder Jeffrey R. Holland stated, "If we persevere, then somewhere in eternity our refinement will be finished and complete—which is the New Testament meaning of *perfection*."[3]

But the Lord doesn't wait for that transformation to be finished before giving us important responsibilities. In fact, He uses us to accomplish His work, *in* our weakness, *with* our weakness, and *despite* our weakness. Somehow, He trusts us right now in our current condition!

Have you ever considered your weakness to be a gift from God to promote humility and growth? How can this change your perspective of who you are and who God knows you can become?

Trust amid Uncertainty

I recently became friends with a remarkable fourteen-year-old young woman from Colorado named Preslee.

I first became acquainted with Preslee when I heard an inspiring message she shared. With Preslee's permission, I'd like to share her message with you.

Preslee was born with cerebral palsy. Her disability restricts many of her physical capabilities, including her ability to walk. Of course, Preslee wishes she could do more. And I'm sure there are moments or even days filled with tears. But Preslee chooses not to let her physical weakness overshadow the strength of her beautiful spiritual gifts or impede her capacity to grow. She understands that the mortal weakness of her body does not determine her divine destiny. I love how Preslee boldly testifies that even with the uncertainty of her future, she has nothing to worry about. She has not quit or even slowed down. She continues to move forward in her faith in Jesus Christ and His Atonement by placing her trust in Him and His promise: "If they . . . have faith in me, then will I make weak things become strong unto them" (Ether 12:27).

Preslee's motto? "I can do hard things!" And she does!

We each face uncertainty and challenges. It's part of our earthly journey. So is weakness. But don't forget—weakness is mortal, but we are divine!

One of the greatest oppositions to moving forward, "notwithstanding [our] weakness" (2 Nephi 33:11), is Satan himself. To stop the work of the Lord from progressing, Satan campaigns diligently to stop *us* from progressing. And he can be pretty good at it. If he can break our inner spirit, bring doubt into our mind, destroy our confidence, or undermine our divine identity, our growth can be stunted.

For the most part, we know our own weak spots. And Satan knows that we know them. Thus, he capitalizes on our insecurities by endeavoring to change our view about our worth. For instance, rather than seeing our God-given weakness as a space to grow, we begin to view it as an impassable barrier. Soon, feelings of hopelessness, inferiority, and worthlessness creep in.

We quit seeing the things we *do imperfectly* as a failure—I failed—and start believing, *I am a failure!*

We no longer see things we do wrong as a mistake—I made a mistake—but embrace the lie, *I am a mistake!*

This type of belief leads to the most catastrophic and crippling form of identity crisis. It prompts additional feelings like:

- I am broken.
- I am nothing.
- I am invisible.
- I am not (whatever) enough.
- I am stuck.
- I am alone.

We cannot bury ourselves in this murky propaganda of the adversary. In all our weakness, we are stronger than he is. We are daughters of divine parentage. Our covenants give us power to overcome such deception. The challenge, however, is remembering who we are.

Now, let's look at how Heavenly Father treats us in our weakness, and even in our mistakes:

- He forgives.
- He assures.
- He encourages.
- He inspires.
- He comforts.
- He strengthens.

With faith and trust in Jesus Christ, we are neither stuck nor alone! He invites us to get in the yoke *with* Him, where He will help us move forward, even if it's only a few inches at a time.

Doctrine of Christ

When I was younger, I used to visualize myself moving through life on an upward line or slope. The more I thought I was doing okay, the more I felt I was going to make it to heaven. But as soon as an unkind word slipped out of my mouth, or I got angry or impatient, I felt myself slide all the way down that slope—hitting rock bottom every time! It was as if all the things I *was* doing right had been erased and I had to start *everything* all over again! I became confident that *I could never be good enough* to make it to the celestial kingdom. It was depressing.

Looking back, I clearly see how I was caught in Satan's pattern of demoralization.

My life changed when I began to understand the doctrine of Christ and how to apply it in my life. I found hope, encouragement, and light. The doctrine of Christ is the Lord's *pattern of change and growth.*

It begins with faith in Jesus Christ and His Atonement. By placing our *faith* and focus on the Savior, we are prompted to grow and make modifications in our lives to become more like Him. We want to repent, grow, and change.

President Russell M. Nelson said, "When we choose to repent, we choose to change!"[4] As we choose to repent, our desire to make and keep covenants with God increases. We choose to be *baptized* and receive the *gift of the Holy Ghost.* The Holy Ghost inspires us to make additional covenants in the temple and *endure to the end.*

Enduring to the end means changing to the end, and so we repeat this continuous cycle of growth throughout our lives. As we continue to apply the doctrine of Christ, we receive His grace, which is the enabling power and spiritual healing offered through the mercy and love of Jesus Christ.

"The grace of God helps us every day. It strengthens us to do [those things] we could not do on our own. The Lord promised that if we humble ourselves before Him and have faith in Him, His grace will help us overcome all our personal weaknesses."[5]

As I continued to follow the pattern in the doctrine of Christ, I began to recognize the good I *was* doing instead of only the failures that seemed to be continually destroying my confidence. I felt empowered. I started to see how each day I could try and be a little better. And when I did give in to weakness, I didn't feel myself tumble the entire way to the ground. Instead of beating myself up, I picked myself up and tried to do better the next time. I grew to *love* the cherished gift of repentance!

This scripture found in Alma 34:31 is one of my favorites about repentance: "If ye will repent and harden not your hearts, *immediately* shall the great plan of redemption be brought about unto you" (Alma 34:31, emphasis added).

The word *immediately* is significant. It does not mean that we will be immediately forgiven. Sometimes that takes time. But when we approach the Lord with a humble and repentant heart, *immediately* He will begin to work within us, and the blessings of His Atonement will flow into our lives. That is a powerful and reassuring promise!

We all make mistakes, and we all need to repent—every day. We cannot become perfect in mortality, but we can be headed in that direction! We can seek to improve each day, showing the Lord our effort to become a little better and more like Him. And we know how the Lord feels about effort!

President Russell M. Nelson taught:

> Because the Savior, through His infinite Atonement, redeemed each of us from weakness, mistakes, and sin, and because He experienced every pain, worry, and burden you have ever had, then as you truly repent and seek His help, you can rise above this present precarious world. . . .
>
> Overcoming the world is not an event that happens in a day or two. It happens over a lifetime as we repeatedly embrace the doctrine of Christ. We cultivate faith in Jesus Christ by repenting daily and keeping covenants that endow us with power. We stay on the covenant path and are blessed with spiritual strength, personal revelation, increasing faith, and the ministering of angels. Living the doctrine of Christ can produce the most powerful virtuous cycle, creating spiritual momentum in our lives.[6]

Slipping into Worthlessness

I admit that I occasionally migrate into that space where "*I am a failure!*" It can be easy to do! And for whatever reason, I feel weakest when I'm fasting.

I attended a sacrament meeting not too long ago in a local

ward. I happened to be fasting and feeling particularly vulnerable. As I looked over the congregation, I beheld a mass of faithful members who had come to partake of the sacrament and worship together. They radiated light and goodness, and I was grateful to be with them. But then out of the blue, that light I had been drawn to suddenly made my light seem very dim. Feelings of total inadequacy quickly and completely filled me—both body and spirit. I felt so small and could not contain my tears. I was embarrassed and closed my eyes as if I was praying, hoping no one would notice. Since my eyes were already closed, I began praying mightily for reassurance and strength. And then the sweetest sound began flowing from the organ.

We began to sing:

> *I know that my Redeemer lives.*
> *What comfort this sweet sentence gives! . . .*
> *He lives to grant me rich supply.*
> *He lives to guide me with his eye.*
> *He lives to comfort me when faint.*
> *He lives to hear my soul's complaint.*
> *He lives to silence all my fears.*
> *He lives to wipe away my tears.*
> *He lives to calm my troubled heart.*
> *He lives all blessings to impart.*[7]

My tears were not wiped away. In fact, they multiplied. But they changed from tears of self-pity to tears of gratitude. Heavenly Father had heard my prayer and had given me a much-needed assurance. He knew where I needed to be that morning to hear His voice through a hymn to calm my troubled heart. Although we are not perfect, we are perfectly known.

Elder Jeffrey R. Holland shared, "The first great *commandment* of all eternity is to love God with all *our* heart, might, mind, and strength—that's the first great commandment. But the first great *truth* of all eternity is that God loves *us* with all of *His* heart, might, mind, and strength."[8]

Negative Space

Sometimes we just need to push away some of the clutter in our lives to bring into focus what matters most. Clutter, whether it's a messy home or a messy schedule, can cause feelings of anxiety and stress and can cloud our ability to recognize the promptings of the Spirit or feel the love of God.

My degree is in interior design. There is a principle in design called negative space. In home design, especially in the field of decorating, there is a tendency to overdecorate, over-prop, and over-fluff—making sure that *every* vertical and *every* horizontal space in the room has something on it! Each item may have special meaning or may have been carefully handpicked, but when *every* space is occupied, the eye does not know where to land. It bounces from wall to wall and from item to item, wondering where to settle. It cannot find the intended focal point.

Negative space is the principle of leaving some areas blank, unadorned, or empty so the positive space, or focal point, is easily noticed.

When we overdecorate our lives with too many "things," it becomes hard to see the focal point—those things of most worth. Our overcrowded lives can leave us physically, emotionally, and spiritually exhausted! In these circumstances, we are more susceptible to feelings of discouragement, self-doubt, and failure. Being overprogrammed, even with good things, makes it difficult for the Holy Ghost to gain our attention. We then miss out on the direction, peace, assurance, and encouragement He offers.

Can we make space for the Lord to fill our hearts? Even a moment of quiet or connection with heaven can refocus us.

Patience and Pace

Since life is neither a race nor a competition, we do not need to run faster or labor more than we have strength.[9] *We can pace our progress.* We can be patient with ourselves and with others.

Elder Neal A. Maxwell gave this wonderful counsel about being patient with ourselves as we progress: "If there were too much swiftness, there could be no long-suffering, no gradual soul-stretching, nor repenting. With too little time to absorb, to assimilate, and to apply the truths already given, our capacities would not be fully developed. Pearls cast before us would go unfound, ungathered, and unsavored. It takes time to prepare for eternity."[10]

Perfectionism

We are not expected to *be* perfect in our mortal state, nor are we expected to *do* everything perfectly. Remember, we are doing many things for the first time in our lives—and I don't just mean our earthly lives!

I'm not really great at anything, but there are many things I love doing. Although we can always strive to do things better and be better, we must work to avoid the "three Cs."

Do not criticize, complain, or compare. We each have our own path and our own pace of growing and learning. We need to give each other and ourselves a much-needed break. In fact, we should compliment, champion, and celebrate our own and each other's progress. And even more, we can show compassion, courage, caring, curiosity, cheer, consideration, and cooperation.

As we offer this generosity to ourselves and others, we will come to know the joy Heavenly Father has in store for us—the same joy that Preslee has found because she chooses to focus on the Savior more than the struggle. We too can focus on Christ more than our weakness. "He is the source of all joy."[11] If we are missing the joy—His joy—in our journey, we are missing everything!

You are magnificent! If you cannot see that, please accept *my certainty* that you are. You are glorious. Your light shines through any dark spaces you may perceive you are in. And when we unite as women bound to the Savior, our light will permeate the world more majestically and brilliantly than all the stars in the heavens.

NOTES

1. Guide to the Scriptures, "Sin," scriptures. ChurchofJesusChrist.org; see also James 4:17.
2. Guide to the Scriptures, "Weakness," scriptures. ChurchofJesusChrist .org.

3. Jeffrey R. Holland, "Be Ye Therefore Perfect—Eventually," *Ensign* or *Liahona*, November 2017.

4. Russell M. Nelson, "We Can Do Better and Be Better," *Ensign* or *Liahona*, May 2019.

5. Gospel Topics, "Grace," topics. ChurchofJesusChrist.org.

6. Russell M. Nelson, "Overcome the World and Find Rest," *Liahona*, November 2022.

7. "I Know That My Redeemer Lives," *Hymns*, no. 136.

8. Jeffrey R. Holland, "Tomorrow the Lord Will Do Wonders among You," *Ensign* or *Liahona*, May 2016.

9. See Doctrine and Covenants 10:4.

10. Neal A. Maxwell, "Meek and Lowly" (Brigham Young University devotional, October 21, 1986), speeches.byu.edu.

11. Russell M. Nelson, "Joy and Spiritual Survival," *Ensign* or *Liahona*, November 2016.

OUR BODIES: ESSENTIAL FOR ETERNAL PROGRESSION AND JOY

Bonnie H. Cordon

As I have traveled around the world, I have been overwhelmed by the love the Lord has for His daughters. I am amazed at the grand contributions you are making to His work. Thank you! We have much to do to help prepare the world for the Lord's coming.

As I have interacted with sisters all over the world, Satan's attacks aimed at our physical bodies have weighed heavily on my mind. Women have always been a target for Satan; he is well aware of the great role we have to play in God's plan. One of the ways he tries to attack us is by persuading women and men to misuse, misunderstand, or minimize the importance of our bodies, relegating women's value to little more than the way we look or our sexual appeal. Both women and men fall prey to these lies.

Elder David A. Bednar taught, "One of the ultimate ironies of eternity is that the adversary, who is miserable precisely because he has no physical body, invites and entices us to share in his misery through the improper use of our bodies. The very tool he does not have and cannot use is thus the primary target of his attempts to lure us to physical *and* spiritual destruction."[1]

The Prophet Joseph Smith summarized that receiving a body is fundamental to our purpose here in mortality: "We came to this earth that we might have a body and present it pure before God in the Celestial Kingdom. The great principle of happiness consists in having a body."[2] That is a bold statement. I pray that we will allow the Holy Ghost to help us more deeply understand some glorious eternal truths about our bodies.

Let's begin with the basics.

Context of the Plan

Before we came to earth, we existed as spirits, children of loving heavenly parents who were then and still are glorified corporeal beings. We desired to become like them—that is, perfect or complete and inheriting in partnership with our spouse "thrones, kingdoms, principalities, and powers, dominions, all heights and depths" (Doctrine and Covenants 132:19). That is no small inheritance. But we were stuck, having progressed as much as we could. Gratefully, our perfect Heavenly Father presented a plan that could make our glorious potential an eternal reality.

Father's plan consisted in each of us choosing to follow Him and His Son, Jesus Christ, first in that realm of spirits and then, if we proved faithful there, coming to earth where our eternal spirit would unite with a physical body, thereby providing us with experiences and opportunities for progression that we could not achieve any other way (see Abraham 3:25–26).

We "shouted for joy" (Job 38:7) at the prospect of such

"earthly learning experiences."[3] We could not wait; we were all in and we said *yes*!

For all who chose to follow God in that first estate—this includes all of us and everyone ever born into the human family—a promised Messiah, Jesus Christ, would sacrifice His own body and blood to ensure the unconditional gift of immortality and the conditional gift of eternal life for each of God's daughters and sons.

And so, here we are in this "next estate" phase of the plan. Perhaps during this mortal journey, you don't always feel like your body brings you great joy or happiness worth shouting for. Truly, physical pain from sickness, abuse, aging, physical limitations, mental illness, and any number of mortal experiences that we face can feel crushing. Emotional and mental distress often accompany such physical challenges and may result from misconstrued perceptions about our bodies as compared to some socially constructed "ideal." This is an especially effective attack against women. We face a near constant barrage of filtered "perfection" and counterfeit messages that our appearance or sexual appeal define our worth.

One or two swipes on your favorite social media app and we are encouraged to look, act, or be like those we see. We have become so accustomed to these messages that we may not even see them anymore, but they seep into our thoughts and perceptions of ourselves and tell us we don't measure up. It can be overwhelming.

Through revealed truth, we know that these views are gross distortions of the true nature and divine need for a body. The Lord revealed in the Doctrine and Covenants that the spirit and the body *together* form the soul, which is such an indispensable union that "the resurrection from the dead *is* the redemption of the soul" (Doctrine and Covenants 88:15–16; emphasis added).

Elder David A. Bednar taught, "The body and the spirit constitute our reality and identity. When body and spirit are inseparably connected, we can receive a fulness of joy; when they are separated, we cannot receive a fulness of joy."[4]

Let's pause for a moment and think about how our spirit and body together—our soul—have helped us experience joy. Take a minute and think of one or two ways you have felt joy because of your body and your spirit.

Do we realize that the joy we experience through our body and spirit is a daily experience? It is a gift and a miracle.

We know that the spirits of those who have died—including our own parents, grandparents, and other loved ones who have left this mortal life—eagerly anticipate their resurrection, as they "[look] upon the . . . absence of their spirits from their bodies as a bondage" (Doctrine and Covenants 138:50). This body that we sometimes find limiting or constraining is the very thing they long for.

Think about the many scriptural phrases where there are references to physical attributes applied in spiritual ways. It would be interesting to note these phrases as you study your scriptures.

We talk about "feeling" the Spirit, being "encircle[d] . . . in the arms of [God's] love" (Doctrine and Covenants 6:20); we are invited to "walk in the meekness of [His] Spirit" (Doctrine and Covenants 19:23) and "put on the whole armor of God" (Ephesians 6:11). We are warned to "touch not the unclean thing" (2 Corinthians 6:17);

the voice of the Lord "pierce[s]" our hearts (3 Nephi 11:3). Perhaps these scriptures would illuminate how our spiritual attributes and growth are enhanced through the joining of our spirits *and* bodies.

There are countless directions we could go when discussing the body: social issues surrounding women's bodies, enduring physical challenges that we face in mortality, or "body image," with all that loaded phrase implies. Please remember, dear friends, that the mortal bodies we have now, which are subject to a fallen world, will one day be raised to immortality. We will live again with these bodies in a glorified state through the atoning blood and bountiful grace of Jesus Christ.

Duality Unlocks Power

Remember Father Lehi's powerful teaching to Jacob that there "must needs be . . . an opposition in all things" (2 Nephi 2:11). Often we think about this opposition in terms of conflict or hostility, where one thing or person is working against the other. But there is also another kind of "opposition" that is critical to our eternal progression. This type of opposition has to do with opposites or contrasts that work *with* rather than *against* each other to fulfill God's purposes.

President Linda Burton gave an example of this type of opposition: "Our two hands are similar to each other but not exactly the same. In fact, they are exact opposites, but they complement each other and are suited to each other. Working together, they are stronger."[5]

Some of my favorite snacks benefit from this same principle. I love the combination of a spicy cinnamon bear dipped in smooth, sweet chocolate, or maybe it is warm cookies accompanied by cold milk.

When you start to think about it, divine complementary contrasts show up frequently in God's plan: bread and water, men and women, birth and death, justice and mercy, the first and the last.

Significantly, in each set of complementary contrasts, one is not more important than the other; rather, both parts are needed and must work together in order to make either one fully efficacious. *It is their duality that unlocks their full power.*

Let's consider for a moment. It is our body and spirit together that participate in ordinances and make covenants with Christ—covenants so vital to our eternal progression that those of us here on earth must stand proxy in the temple for those same sacred ordinances on behalf of our deceased ancestors.

It is only in the eternal pairing of our bodies and spirits that we and they can achieve our full potential and inherit eternal life. Working together, our bodies and spirits unlock greater access to power and potential than either has on its own.[6]

Christ "In the Flesh"

Let's consider the example of the Savior. It is clear from the scriptures that Christ's saving Atonement had to be carried out "in the flesh" (2 Nephi 9:5). In order to satisfy the demands of justice and provide the Savior with the power to cleanse and exalt us, it was, of necessity, a combined physical and spiritual experience.[7]

Alma, in one of the most stirring sermons, teaches, "And

[Christ] shall go forth, suffering pains and afflictions and temptations of every kind; . . . he will take upon him the pains and the sicknesses of his people. And he will take upon him death, that he may loose the bands of death which bind his people; and he will take upon him their infirmities, that his bowels may be filled with mercy, *according to the flesh*, that he may know *according to the flesh* how to succor his people according to their infirmities" (Alma 7:11–12; emphasis added).

And then this beautiful truth: "Now the Spirit knoweth all things; nevertheless the Son of God suffereth *according to the flesh* that he might take upon him the sins of his people, that he might blot out their transgressions according to the power of his deliverance" (Alma 7:13; emphasis added).

It was not until and it was only when the spirit Jehovah—who had created the world and parted the Red Sea and been with the Father from the beginning—was combined with a physical, tangible body as Jesus Christ that His ultimate power was realized.

This significant truth is one of the reasons why, in the sacrament, Christ invites us to remember the power wrought by the sacrifice of His *body* and His *blood*, freely offered in willing submission to His Father.[8] This physical sacrifice and an equally weighty spiritual suffering—Jesus Himself described His suffering to be in "both body and spirit"—was *required* to "unlock the gate of heav'n and let us in."[9]

By Their Own Experience

Like the Savior, we need to learn by our own experience how to use our bodies. We all love to give advice to those who are approaching milestones that we have already faced. We say to first-time expectant parents, "Get your sleep in now!" We recall to newly set-apart missionaries, "It will be the hardest and greatest time of your life!"

The same principle applies in all aspects of our growth and knowledge: trying to convey to others the magnitude of our experience is inadequate; to truly *know*, we have to experience it for ourselves.[10]

These mortal experiences prepare us for immortality and try our very limits physically, emotionally, even spiritually. It is in union and harmony of our body and spirit working together toward God's righteous purposes that we are able to withstand the soul-stretching experience of mortality. It takes our physical bodies together with our spirits.

Do you see how this is an eternal principle? In the realm of spirits we had already advanced as far as we could; to continue to progress, we would need the experience of our fabulous but flawed bodies to ultimately become like our heavenly parents. We couldn't just listen to or study their experiences of having physical bodies; we had to get them for ourselves.

A united spirit and physical body unlock greater access to power and potential than either have on their own.[11]

Consider that Satan's punishment for rebelling against the Father was to never receive a body. Is it any wonder then that Satan targets our bodies so viciously in his attacks? He will never experience the power, potential, and joy that you can. Literally, he cannot. He will not ever become what you can, and that must be infuriatingly final. He will never hold a new baby in his arms or hug a beloved grandparent or friend. Indeed, when being "cast out by the Savior," the unclean spirits "asked to go into the herd of swine, showing that [they] prefer [even] a swine's body to having none."[12]

In his desire that we be as miserable as he is, the adversary seeks to undermine and minimize the great power that we have, or else tempt us to misuse that power in ways that are contrary to the laws of God, thus creating the same misery for us that he dwells within. If he has to be miserable, so should we.

Power of Touch

As I've studied the Savior's life in the New Testament, I, like you, have loved reading of His miracles: His expressions of mercy and compassion toward those who sought to be healed.

Isn't it amazing that the Savior's power to heal was not dependent on His physical proximity to the afflicted? Many times, the Lord simply speaks a word and the miracle rolls forth.[13]

It is instructive then that so often the Lord chose to incorporate physical touch into His miracles: He touched sightless eyes, anointed them with clay, or applied saliva. In the healing of one deaf and dumb, the Lord put His fingers into the man's ears and touched his tongue. He took Jairus's daughter by the hand to call her back to life. If strictly unnecessary for His power to be effective, why would He choose to accompany many of His healings with a physical touch?

His physical touch, in conjunction with His power to heal, provided additional depth that assisted these individuals not just in being whole, but in knowing and loving Him as the Christ.

There is a powerful connection that comes from the gentle, *safe* touch of those who love us: a hug, holding hands, a grandmother or aunt brushing your hair.

There is science to back up our need for physical connection. Oxytocin is known as the "cuddle" or "love hormone" because it is a chemical that is released when you snuggle up to someone. An article about the benefits of hugging pointed out that "we are meant to be held, we are meant to socialize. . . . Your family needs hand to hand, eye-to-eye, body-to-body-contact."[14]

Several years ago, I learned about the emotional and physical power of an eight-second hug. This is something I tried with my adult son. When I first asked him to hug me for eight seconds, he gave me that look (you know the look), but now, it is something that helps us both feel loved, calm, and connected.

Researchers have found these same effects from "a pat on the back, a high-five, a brush on the shoulder, even eye to eye contact—any form of positive physical and social connection—counts. What really matters is that we are making the effort to connect . . . that we are letting [those around us] know through our attention and actions that we love them, that they aren't alone, and that they are valued."[15]

Sometimes, words fail us and what we need, or the best we can give, is a loving touch.

In 3 Nephi 11, Jesus Christ models the importance of physical touch with his invitation:

> Arise and come forth unto me, that ye may *thrust* your
> hands into my side, and also that ye may feel the prints of

the nails in my hands and in my feet, that ye may *know* that I am . . . the God of the whole earth, and have been slain for the sins of the world.

And . . . the multitude went forth, and thrust their hands into his side, and did feel the prints of the nails in his hands and in his feet . . . one by one . . . and did see with their eyes and did feel with their hands, and did know of a surety and did bear record, that it was he. (3 Nephi 11:14–16; emphasis added)

He knew that the best way to cement His relationship with people and to solidify their love for and knowledge of Him was through close, inspired, individual connection—the unity of the spirit and the body working in harmony to accomplish God's purposes. He only then proceeded to teach them, heal them, and bless them.

His Instruments

Can we not emulate the Savior's perfect example in this?

So much of what we do as women is physically oriented. All women have a divine mandate to nurture God's children who are within our sphere.[16] Often that nurturing, ministering work is physically demanding. But feed, clothe, clean, bandage, wash, repeat should not be menial temporal tasks![17] They are precisely what the Lord did during His mortal sojourn. When done with gentleness, meekness, love, and intention, these are the very things that build strong relationships and lead us all to Christ.

President Henry B. Eyring has taught, "Never, never underestimate the spiritual value of doing temporal things well for those whom you serve."[18] As we are more purposeful and thoughtful in seeking the guidance of the Spirit in our daily interactions, we will witness miracles, even spiritual ones.

Be Present

The rich connection that God intends for us and that is enhanced in our physical bodies is not just about the touch itself—though that is a key component. It is about being present—deeply seeing those around us.

Sister Michelle Craig taught:

> Jesus Christ sees people deeply. He sees individuals, their needs, and who they can become. Where others saw fishermen, sinners, or publicans, Jesus saw disciples; where others saw a man possessed by devils, Jesus looked past the outward distress, acknowledged the man, and healed him.
>
> Even in our busy lives, we can follow the example of Jesus and see individuals—their needs, their faith, their struggle, and who they can become.[19]

Being present and connecting in real ways is increasingly vital in our digital world. Technology can be a blessing, but there are reasons for concern.

Have you had the experience of visiting with a friend or talking with a family member when their phone has "dinged" with an email or text that they immediately read? Have you had the experience of sitting in a school class, church meeting, or work function where you miss what is happening in front of you because you are checking every buzz or news headline that pops up?

Do you see how this is a devious attempt by Satan to "[entice] embodied spirits to forfeit the blessings and learning experiences 'according to the flesh' (1 Nephi 19:6; Alma 7:12–13) that are made possible through the Father's plan of happiness and the Atonement of His Only Begotten Son"?[20]

Contrast that with the experience of looking into the eyes of someone during a meaningful conversation, laughing with your family or friends around the dinner table, feeling the warmth of the sunshine during your favorite hike, or reading scriptures with your grandson or niece.

While there is great value that can come from connecting with others through technology, we need to make sure that we are also having personal, physical connections with one another. These *real-life* experiences will become ever more vital as the wonders of artificial intelligence and virtual reality increase. Be present and make a difference in the lives of others. Don't talk yourself out of opportunities to connect just because you have to change out of your sweats. Go to the ward activity. Gather with friends. Even if there is an awkward moment or two, it is one of the most exhilarating ways the Father intended for us to experience joy.

Invitation and Promise

I plead with you to recognize the glorious gift of your physical body and the power you have when your spirit and body work together to further God's purposes. Our bodies are so much more than a temporary box to house our spirits—a box to decorate and display without impact. Can you see why we continue to teach the sanctity of the body, the need for chastity, the blessing of modesty, and the necessity to tend and care for our physical bodies?

President Russell M. Nelson taught pure truth when he said, "The gift of our physical bodies is a transcendent miracle. A unique body is given to each of us by our loving Heavenly Father. He created it . . . to assist each of us in our quest to fulfill the full measure of our creation."[21]

I hope you will absorb all of your soul-stretching experiences in this mortal realm and allow them to deepen, enhance, and accelerate your preparation for the promised realms of glory.

I want to echo Elder Bednar's promise that "these eternal truths about the importance of our physical bodies will fortify you against the deception and the attacks of the adversary. . . . I testify that God lives and is our Heavenly Father. . . . Jesus is the Christ, the Redeemer, whose body was bruised, broken, and torn for us as He offered His atoning sacrifice. He is resurrected, [and] He lives. . . . To be 'encircled about eternally in the arms of his love' (2 Nephi 1:15) will be a real and not a virtual experience."[22]

Christ is our hope and our peace as we seek to follow Him.

NOTES

1. David A. Bednar, "Things as They Really Are," *Ensign* or *Liahona*, June 2010; emphasis added.
2. "Discourse, 5 January 1841, as Reported by William Clayton," 7–8, *The Joseph Smith Papers*, josephsmithpapers.org.
3. Bednar, "Things as They Really Are."
4. Bednar, "Things as They Really Are."
5. Linda K. Burton, "We'll Ascend Together," *Ensign* or *Liahona*, May 2015, 30.

6. See "Discourse, 30 January 1842," 4, *The Joseph Smith Papers*, josephsmithpapers.org.

7. See Doctrine and Covenants 19:18.

8. See Matthew 26:26–28.

9. "There Is a Green Hill Far Away," *Hymns*, no. 194.

10. See Jan E. Newman, "Teaching in the Savior's Way," *Liahona*, May 2021.

11. See "Discourse, 30 January 1842," 4, *The Joseph Smith Papers*, josephsmithpapers.org.

12. *Teachings of Presidents of the Church: Joseph Smith* (2007), 211.

13. See, for example, the centurion's servant (Matthew 8:5–13) or the nobleman's son (John 4:46–54).

14. Christy Kane, in Travis Barton, "Hugs Are Better for Your Brain than Electronics, Says Expert," *Riverton Journal*, December 11, 2018, rivertonjournal.com.

15. Morgan Young, "The Value of a Hug: One Important Thing You Can Do for Your Child Today," *Medium*, April 24, 2019, medium.com.

16. See "The Family: A Proclamation to the World," ChurchofJesusChrist .org.

17. See Julie B. Beck, "Mothers Who Know," *Ensign* or *Liahona*, November 2007.

18. Henry B. Eyring, "The Book of Mormon Will Change Your Life," *Ensign* or *Liahona*, February 2004.

19. Michelle D. Craig," Eyes to See," *Ensign* or *Liahona*, November 2020.

20. Bednar, "Things as They Really Are."

21. Russell M. Nelson, "Your Body: A Magnificent Gift to Cherish," *New Era*, August 2019.

22. Bednar, "Things as They Really Are."

WHATEVER MY LOT . . .
IT IS WELL WITH MY SOUL

Jennie Taylor

Some years ago, I received a phone call from my mom, who was with my children at my North Ogden home. She told me there were two United States Army officers in full dress uniform on my front porch and they had something important to tell me. Something, they said, that could only be said in person.

Those Army officers had been sent to tell me that my husband, Major Brent Taylor, had been killed in action outside of Kabul, Afghanistan.

I, like you, have had goals and dreams and failures and successes. I, like you, have found myself downright shocked at the plot twists of my life. And I, like you—like everyone who has ever lived on this earth—have great need of the love, grace, and mercy of our Savior, Jesus Christ.

We will inevitably run into plot twists along the way. Each time we discover such a plot twist, we can decide whether we will let it be a stumbling block or a stepping stone. When we choose to step forward in spite of life's challenges, we would be wise to remember that Jesus is "the way, the truth, and the life" (John 14:6), and that in Him and through Him and because of Him we can come unto the Father.

In Doctrine and Covenants 59:23, Christ promises us "peace in this world, and eternal life in the world to come." These blessings are not only eternal (or eventual), but are intended by our loving Savior Jesus Christ to be ours *now*. A well-known reminder of that truth is found in 2 Nephi 2:25, which tells us, "men are, that they might have joy."

So how do we do it? How do we experience the peace that frees us from our daily distresses so we can live true lives of joy?

Enter here the three Ts: trials, truth, and trust.

Let's start with trials. I am positive all of us have a list of trials we have either experienced ourselves or seen in the lives of people we know and love. In fact, if you have a piece of paper, go ahead and actually make the list. But if not, you can make the list in your mind. Start from long ago and add your trials up to today.

What would your list of trials look like? What would your list of trials feel like? And what good would that list do you?

Odds are, the trials you've experienced have been heartbreaking and difficult. Sometimes they've been large and sometimes they've been small. Some have been shared and some have been walked alone.

On my list, I could include the repeated times my parents moved our family during my early elementary school years, or my memories of my parents' marriage ending and my father's death by suicide. My list could include my brothers' struggles with drugs and alcohol. I might mention the challenges of pregnancy and childbirth, the exhaustion of motherhood and homemaking, and the added layer of difficulty in raising a family with a husband who repeatedly went away to war.

I could write of my husband's youngest brother's death by suicide in 2011—when that youngest brother wasn't quite sixteen. I'd include my husband's fourth combat deployment in 2018, which would, of course, lead to that knock on the door from those two Army officers sent to notify me of my husband's death.

My list could go on. And so could yours.

Your list won't look exactly like mine, or like the lists any other women you know might make. There's no need to compete or compare when it comes to chronicling our challenges in life. We've all faced plenty of trials. But let's not stop with just that list.

So together, let's move on to the second T: truth.

Let's take that same list we made of our trials and fold the paper in half. It's okay if you're creating an imaginary list—just make sure that mental list has two sides. I invite you to take a good look at each trial on the left and think of at least one corresponding truth to write on the right—a truth you have learned, relearned, or come to understand with greater depth because of that trial. There is power to be found in discovering the Savior and His loving gospel truths *in* our trials, not just *after* them or *despite* them.

Could you find the truth in your trials? What would that list look like? What would that list feel like? And what good would that list of truths do you?

I've spent years as a wife, a mother, and a devoted disciple of Jesus Christ, and I'll admit that I thought I knew what truth was. I've read the scriptures. I've prayed in faith. I've felt the power of the Holy Ghost. But when I take a closer look at the course of my life and the truths that I know, I cannot deny that I have learned the depths of those truths through times of great trial.

Perhaps for you, the parallel list comes quickly. You can see the trial written on the left and easily identify the truth learned on the right. Or maybe you are struggling, feeling guilty, or second-guessing yourself because you don't think you know as many truths as you're "supposed" to know.

Maybe right now, that list on the left is so long and so daunting that you're not sure you can even find a thing to write down on the right. Perhaps you can remember at some distant point knowing some element of truth, and yet right now you are so enveloped in darkness and despair that you're not sure you even remember what it feels like to know anything for sure. I know what that's like. Though my husband had served for fifteen years in the Army and been deployed to hazardous combat zones four times, his death came as a shock to us all. It was a trial that left us all grasping for truth.

May I share with you a scripture that one of my brothers-in-law shared at my husband's funeral? In 1 Nephi 11:17, Nephi admits that even he, a righteous son of a prophet who was also a prophet himself, does "not know the meaning of all things."

Nevertheless, Nephi testifies in the very same verse that he knows the Lord loves His children.

If you are struggling to make a list of all the truths you know or could know or think you "should" know, please let go of all "shoulds" and try to let yourself come to know of the immediate goodness of God. Try to let yourself turn from your trials to even the tiniest of truths. As you do, I am confident you will find that recognizing even one simple truth will help you come to recognize countless others.

Let me share an example from my childhood. Hindsight and the Holy Ghost have given me a vantage point where I can now see a myriad of truths that I've learned through the tragedy of losing my father at far too young an young age. That myriad of truths began with the hope that one truth I had been taught was actually true: in the wake of my father's death, I wanted very much to see him again.

That desire lined up nicely with what my mother and my primary teachers had been saying—and even singing—for years about families being together forever. I really wanted that truth to be true. So, I let that desire grow. In time, my desire to believe in eternal families led to an awareness of the importance of sacred and holy temples, which led to a belief in the power and authority of the priesthood, which helped me gain a testimony of the leaders of the Church who held that priesthood.

Coming to know for myself that the Lord had called a living prophet led me to recognize the truth and divinity of the Prophet Joseph Smith's call, which helped me recognize the truth and divinity of the teachings he translated from the gold plates, which helped me come to know that modern revelation—even personal revelation—is real and readily available. This knowledge has helped me make countless decisions and move forward through trials large and small.

So if you are struggling to complete your parallel list of truths, may I invite you to please search for one truth first. Plant the seed of faith in that one truth, and then move forward in that faith so that it can blossom and grow and help you come to know, "line upon line, precept upon precept, here a little and there a little" (2 Nephi 28:30), through the power of God and the gift of the Holy Ghost.

Remember the great promise found in the Book of Mormon: "And by the power of the Holy Ghost ye may know the truth of all things" (Moroni 10:5).

That leads me to the third and final T: trust.

As we turn to truth in our times of trials, we will come to more naturally—and more fully—trust in Christ. We can trust Him who has promised us peace in this world and eternal life in the world to come, because He lived a life that was perfectly trustworthy. He promises to send us a peace that passeth all understanding.

So maybe one step we each need to take is to let go of the insistence that we understand everything. We can know truth and still not understand all that God understands.[1] That's why faith is the first principle of the gospel. And it's also why agency is so essential: because we can use our agency to choose to trust in Christ. We can trust that though our understanding is limited by our mortality, He truly knows all things.[2] And He has promised that *all things* shall work together for our good.

My husband was killed on a Saturday morning. Sometime Sunday evening, I was standing in my bedroom when a thought very clearly came into my mind. The thought was, "This will be good for me."

And it continued, "This will be good for my family. This will be good for us."

Christ long ago declared the promise that all things shall work together for our good, for those of us who strive to "search diligently, pray always, and be believing" (Doctrine and Covenants 90:24).

Mere hours after learning of my husband's death, I was faced with a choice: the choice to trust. It is a choice I made with massive effort and what felt like immeasurable faith. In the time since, I cannot tell you how many times I have leaned on the truth that all things really will work together for our good.

Alma the Younger taught his son Helaman that "whosoever shall put their trust in God shall be supported in their trials, and their troubles, and their afflictions" (Alma 36:3). The ability to trust comes when we turn to the truths we do know, or even to the truths we hope to know. We do not need to know everything in order to know enough.[3] Perhaps it is enough to simply know we can trust Jesus Christ.

Take heart in the three Ts—trials, truth, and trust. Take the time to make the list of your trials and the corresponding truths you have learned therein. Come to know you can trust the Savior. And then continually make the choice to do so.

In Doctrine and Covenants 19:23, the Savior says, "Learn of me, and listen to my words; walk in the meekness of my Spirit, and you shall have peace in me."

The Savior has both commanded and invited us to learn, listen, and walk. He wants us to face our trials with our testimonies of truth and to more fully trust in Him.

We can learn of Him through daily scripture study. We can listen to His words in the temple and in the teachings of living prophets. We can listen to His Holy Spirit as we pray and strive to live our lives the way He would have us live. And we can walk in His light and with His love when we put one foot in front of the other and look for ways to help others navigate their own trials.

As we accept Christ's invitation to learn, listen, and walk, He promises that we will have peace in Him. I know that truths can sustain us in our trials. I know that Christ is perfectly worthy of our trust. May you choose to act in faith and more fully come to trust in the Savior.

NOTES

1. See Mosiah 4:9.
2. See 2 Nephi 9:20.
3. See Neil L. Andersen, "You Know Enough," *Ensign* or *Liahona*, November 2008.

BRINGING HIS RELIEF

Camille N. Johnson,
J. Anette Dennis, Kristin M. Yee

Camille N. Johnson: On March 17, 1842, the day the Relief Society was organized, Emma Smith's counselors moved that the Society be called "The Nauvoo Female Relief Society."[1] Elder John Taylor offered an amendment that it be called The Nauvoo Female *Benevolent* Society.

Emma and Eliza R. Snow explained that "benevolent" was a popular word—popular with the institutions of the day—but that popular should not be our guide.[2] Emma expounded that the word *relief* better described their mission and said, "We are going to do something extraordinary . . . we expect extraordinary occasions and pressing calls."[3]

The sisters' explanation was compelling and so they were organized as the *Relief* Society.[4] We remain the *Relief* Society. As President Dallin H. Oaks has taught, "[We are] not just a class for women but something [we] belong to—a divinely established appendage to the priesthood."[5]

And so, as sisters and friends, we stand ready to provide re-lief—expecting extraordinary occasions and pressing calls.

As members of the Relief Society, we point one another to the Savior for *relief* and follow the Savior's example in giving Christlike love. We provide *relief*—temporal and spiritual—through the power of the Savior and in the process find our own relief. We find Jesus Christ.

Kristin M. Yee: Finding relief through our covenant relation-ship with God has been on my mind and heart for some time. As the prophet of the Lord has taught and exhorted us to learn about covenants, temples, and priesthood power, I've found my-self searching, loving, and feasting upon the rejuvenating truths encapsulated in covenants.

We were meant to partner with the Lord in a powerful way through our covenants. He desires to be with us in our concerns and our decisions. We need not navigate the challenges, sorrows, insecurities, and heartaches of life alone. He will be beside us. He has said, "I will not leave you comfortless: I will come to you" (John 14:18). President Russell M. Nelson described the char-acter of God and His great love for us when he taught that "the covenant path is all about our relationship with God."

He also said, "All those who have made a covenant with God have access to a special kind of love and mercy. In the Hebrew language, that covenantal love is called *hesed* (חֶסֶד). . . . Because God has *hesed* for those who have covenanted with Him, He will love them. He will continue to work with them and offer them opportunities to change. He will forgive them when they repent.

And should they stray, He will help them find their way back to Him.

"Once you and I have made a covenant with God, our relationship with Him becomes much closer than before our covenant. Now we are bound together. Because of our covenant with God, He will never tire in His efforts to help us, and we will never exhaust His merciful patience with us. Each of us has a special place in God's heart. He has high hopes for us."[6]

As a sister who has not yet married, I know this loving and merciful covenant relationship with my Father in Heaven and Savior has a powerful place in my life and is my greatest source of relief and peace. It brings me unspeakable comfort, divine joy, and a deep abiding assurance that I am loved as His daughter, and that I belong to His eternal family. I know that He knows me and understands me *completely*.

No matter our marital status or background, the Lord desires us to partner with Him in a powerful way. To be "one"[7] with Him in "all [our] doings."[8]

Our thoughts and actions reflect the relationships we value. Hence, the more we love God and value our covenant relationship with Him, the more we will become as He is. And we will receive of His joy, peace, purpose, and power.

As we cry unto the Lord for our support, and "let the affections of [our] heart[s] be placed upon [Him] forever" (Alma 37:36), our lives can be filled by this beautiful covenant bond.

Through our Savior Jesus Christ, we can receive relief from navigating the challenges of life alone.

We all have concerns and needs that we can feel alone in, but He cares about our concerns no matter how great or small. I have felt the need for His help when worrying about seemingly small things like the ever-present friend I call "house repairs." Without a spouse to consult with, I can worry alone about the right contractor, fair costs, taking time away from work to be home, and being a good steward over my finances and home. It was a triumph the other day to get my garage door fixed! The Lord heard my concern. And though small in the grand scheme of things, He answered my prayer. How? Through a kind neighbor, the help of the Spirit, and a video on YouTube, I was blessed to know what to do to fix the door.

I have felt His love and relief in my personal needs and concerns. He has provided healing, wisdom, and strength beyond my own. Through the power of His Atoning Sacrifice, He has lovingly supplied help and compensatory blessings. And often He sends that help and relief through the hands of others.

If the Lord is attentive to the small needs, imagine His desire to bless and sustain us in the weightier matters of the heart and soul, which are not few in number—difficult family relationships; loss and disappointment; ongoing mental and physical health challenges; abuse; constant concern as a parent; constant concern in caring for a parent, wayward child or spouse; or struggles with personal faith, financial distress, and addiction. Our Father in Heaven knew we would need a Savior to provide relief and to save us from physical and spiritual death, sorrow and sin. And so, He sent His Beloved Son.

During the intensities and infirmities of life, I've leaned heavily upon and held closely to my covenant relationship with God. As I've trusted in His loving care and tried my best to consecrate my life to Him, He has provided relief through His priesthood power and has been my Provider in my spiritual and temporal needs. He has provided relief from fear, relief from insecurities, relief from pride, relief from sin, relief from loneliness, relief from sorrow.

President Nelson taught with clarity and assurance that "the reward for keeping covenants with God is heavenly power—power that strengthens us to withstand our trials, temptations, and heartaches better."[9]

Through Jesus Christ, we can receive relief from navigating the challenges of life alone.

As I've been reflecting on the blessings of the "covenant bond"[10] we have with God, I thought about my recent assignment to the Asia North Area.

I had the privilege of traveling to the small islands of Chuuk in Micronesia, about 1,500 miles southeast of Japan. Upon arrival, you could almost feel a spirit of heaviness. Poverty was prevalent, along with violence, sorrow, and many other hardships. But amidst these difficult circumstances, there was the bright light of faith—a small band of Saints that continued to strive to keep their covenants.

On one of the smaller islands without running water or electricity, a beautiful sister shared that it had been forty years since the missionaries found her and she joined the Church. When

I met her, she was praying to one day have her husband, who struggled with alcohol, attend the temple with her. She testified of the blessings of eternal marriage and the temple.

This sister knew her Heavenly Father, and though she was "alone" on a little island of the sea, she was *not* alone. God had been with her. She held fast to her covenants with Him. Her relationship with Him has carried her and has been a comfort to her.

On Weno, Chuuk, two of the sisters in the Relief Society have given their lives to raise children that have been abandoned by their parents. These two sisters felt it was important to raise these children in the gospel. One of these sisters is single and working full-time as a school counselor. I shared with them President Nelson's message to the sisters of the Church, which is that we sisters are loved, necessary, and precious.[11]

The beautiful single sister, who is raising her nieces and nephews, broke down in tears and said she had not felt precious lately. She had felt forgotten. But she testified she felt of God's love and awareness for her in the prophet's words that she was indeed "precious," and she knew it was true. She felt God's healing love; she felt relief.

Remember the Lord's question: "Know ye not that I, the Lord your God, have created all men, and that I remember those who are upon the isles of the sea?" (2 Nephi 29:7).

These sisters are known to their Heavenly Father and Savior; they are not alone. And neither are you and I in our trials and challenges. The Lord sent me roughly 8,500 miles by plane, train, car, and boat to bring God's love and relief to "the one"[12] on the isles of the sea. And so, He will find you and me on our personal islands where we might feel alone in the concerns and the burdens we carry in our hearts. He is present and prepared to bless, guide, and comfort us.

Our covenant bond with Him is our strength and our joy. In the words of Isaiah: "God is my salvation; I will trust, and not be afraid: for the Lord Jehovah is my strength and my song" (Isaiah 12:2). I testify that He is aware of you and knows your heart. He loves you.

In 1 Nephi we read the Lord's words from Isaiah: "But, behold, Zion hath said: The Lord hath forsaken me, and my Lord hath forgotten me. . . . Can a woman forget her sucking child, that she should not have compassion on the son of her womb? Yea, they may forget, yet will I not forget thee. . . . Behold, I have graven thee upon the palms of my hands; thy walls are continually before me" (1 Nephi 21:14–16).

Your concerns, your desires, your worries, and your interests are continually before Him. He has "graven thee upon the palms of [His] hands" (1 Nephi 21:16, Isaiah 49:16). There is never a time you are not on the forefront of His mind and in His heart. He sees you. And He *will* come to your aid. He will comfort your heart with His healing love and assurance.

President Gordon B. Hinckley once described the experience of a young divorced "mother of seven children, then ranging in ages from 7 to 16. She said that one evening she went across the street to deliver something to a neighbor." These are her words as he recalled them.

As I turned around to walk back home, I could see my house lighted up. I could hear echoes of my children as I had walked out of the door a few minutes earlier. They were saying: "Mom, what are we going to have for dinner?" "Can you take me to the library?" "I have to get some poster paper tonight." Tired and weary, I looked at that house and saw the light on in each of the rooms. I thought of all of those children who were home waiting for me to come and meet their needs. My burdens felt heavier than I could bear.

I remember looking through tears toward the sky, and I said, "Dear Father, I just can't do it tonight. I'm too tired. I can't face it. I can't go home and take care of all those children alone. Could I just come to You and stay with You for just one night?" . . .

I didn't really hear the words of reply, but I heard them in my mind. The answer was: "No, little one, you can't come to me now. . . . But I can come to you."[13]

He came to her, and He will come to you and me, just as the Savior came to the woman at the well where she labored and toiled through her days.[14] He came to her. He encouraged her, taught her, declared His Messiahship to her, and loved her when perhaps she didn't love herself. To the woman at the well, to the young mother of seven, to you and me, Jesus Christ stands ready to provide relief. I testify that we can receive relief through our covenant bond with a loving God.

As we trust in God, we will feel of His great love and care, and come to know Him in ways we would never otherwise know Him.

Perhaps like me, you have pled for help to not be left alone during some of the most emotionally, physically, and spiritually demanding seasons of your life. These intense seasons of growth have left what I call "spiritual stretch marks" on the soul. But I bear witness that He has carried me, and He will carry you. He has graven you upon the palms of His hands. He has been there as you've sought "to be righteous in the dark."[15] He has not forsaken me, nor will He forsake you.[16] And I will love Him forever for it.

I testify that Jesus Christ is relief.[17] He desires to care for you, to bless and forgive you. He came for this very purpose, to provide you with the much-needed relief that you seek. He is the Redeemer of the world and I testify that He lives, and that He loves you.

J. Anette Dennis: President Russell M. Nelson said, "It is my conviction that our Savior can strengthen and enable us to reach our highest highs and be able to cope with our lowest lows. As an ordained Apostle of Jesus Christ, I invite you to seek to know for yourself that He is the Master Healer."[18]

I have been a witness to the kind and gentle ways the Savior provides relief, as well as to His power as the Master Healer over the past five years of my daughter Sarah's sacred healing journey.

Sarah began showing signs of anxiety before she was two years old. We thought the anxiety might be due to the medical tests she was put through because of the gastrointestinal reflux condition she had suffered since birth.

As she grew into adolescence, we blamed her distress on teenage hormonal changes and her highly sensitive nature. Because of her sensitive nature, she was always very attuned to the pain of others and often looked for ways to help others feel better, but she usually suffered her own pain alone.

In early 2018, while we were serving in the temple in Ecuador, Sarah's distress became so intense that she became suicidal. This was a very dark time for her, and especially difficult for us because we were so far away. She was taken to the hospital, and we flew home for several weeks to be with her. We seriously considered not returning, but in response to our prayers, the Lord's answer was that if we would just trust Him and return to Ecuador, He would be able to help Sarah much more quickly than if we stayed.

It was one of the hardest things we've ever done to get on that plane and fly back to Ecuador. But because Sarah went to live with our son and his wife, who is a nurse, our daughter-in-law observed things in Sarah she hadn't seen before and shared those observations with her mother, who was an AP Psychology teacher. Because of her background and knowledge, she had some very important insights that later led to the diagnosis of a condition my husband and I had never heard of.

This condition had caused Sarah to feel easily rejected and unloved by others. This often took the form of feeling rejected and abandoned by her Father in Heaven and feeling certain that He loved all His other daughters but didn't love her. This was evidenced in her mind by the perceived happiness others had in their lives and the pain and suffering she had in hers. Her self-rejection and self-hate were so painful to watch, and I cried to the Lord on many occasions, pleading with Him to take away her suffering.

Soon after that diagnosis, we found a specialized therapy and, just four months after we had gotten on that plane to return to Ecuador, the Lord told us that now it was time to go home and walk beside Sarah on her journey of healing. Because of the great blessing of that early diagnosis, Sarah was able to begin learning skills that helped her deal with the overwhelming feelings of distress and strong emotions the condition caused her.

It has been a long and difficult journey, but over the years as she learned to deal with the emotional pain and distress in healthier ways, Sarah began to see the Lord's hand in her life. She began to feel her Heavenly Father's love for her and to feel greater love and acceptance for herself. We have watched in amazement over these past five years as we have witnessed the Lord's healing power in Sarah's life, gradually giving her much-needed emotional relief.

During the most difficult times, there were particular verses of scripture the Lord led me to that brought peace and relief to my heart each time I read them.

One of those was 2 Nephi 8:3. I found comfort in replacing the word "Zion" with Sarah's name: "For the Lord shall comfort [Sarah]; he will comfort all her waste places; and he will make her wilderness like Eden, and her desert like the garden of the Lord. Joy and gladness shall be found therein, thanksgiving and the voice of melody."

Recently I was invited to speak at a Family Services conference, and I asked Sarah if she would share her feelings about

Christ's role in her ongoing journey of healing. With her permission, I will share part of it:

> In looking back over my journey of healing so far, I think I am only just now coming to . . . understand how present and actively involved Jesus Christ was in my life. . . .
>
> The Savior has been personally ministering to me throughout my whole life, yet in waiting for some grand and unusual witness of God's love for me, I neglected to see the signs of my Savior's love that were all around. It wasn't until late last year when I was taking an institute class about symbolism and the Atonement that the reality of my Savior and His part in my healing journey . . . began to feel tangible to me.
>
> As we talked about the Savior and the symbols of His life and sacrifice, our institute teacher turned us to the symbol of motherhood and to the idea of the Savior as a mother. Isaiah 49:15–16 says, "Can a woman forget her sucking child, that she should not have compassion on the son of her womb? Yea, they may forget, yet will I not forget thee. Behold, I have graven thee upon the palms of my hands." . . .
>
> "Oh, so my Savior is like my mom," I thought. He is my defender, my advocate, my therapist, my comforter, my teacher, and in so many ways, my healer. [Since understanding this], I have begun to feel that I can move forward in my life with more confidence . . . and I have looked into my past with new gratitude.
>
> In all my days of suffering, my Savior had been right beside me, ministering to me through the people who loved

me. He was there through my mother, who cried with me when neither of us knew what to do or what to try next and when I needed to feel covered by the wing of a parent's love.

He was there through my Primary teacher who spent extra time with me, answering my questions and visiting with me as an equal. . . .

He was there through my friend and my friend's parents who came to visit me and minister to me before I was admitted to the hospital for the first time. . . .

He was there through my college math teacher, [who called] to tell me that he'd noticed I was not in class and [asked me] to let him know if there was anything I needed or that he could do. He was willing to work with me and help me get caught up.

He was there through my therapist and psychologist [who taught] me and [shared] truth with me, which set the wheels in motion for . . . me to comprehend that [Christ] could love someone so flawed and so imperfect and small as I was. . . .

It makes sense to me now that to know and to have a relationship with Jesus Christ is to know that I am safe to go and do whatever He asks of me. To know my Savior is to know help will always come. To know my Savior is to know that I can stand tall and be confident in whatever company I am in when I am truly repentant and my heart is pure. To know my Savior is to . . . take refuge in the knowledge that He can see my heart and my progress even when no one else can. To know my Savior means that I do not have to be ashamed for the mistakes and shortcomings of my past or hide myself in the shadow of others' judgments. To know my Savior is to know that I am not and will never be alone.

Christ is the embodiment of newness and rebirth, and no matter how torn and tattered I feel from being knocked around in the rock tumbler of life, through Him I can be reborn and become new again, and I have. He has been with me every step of the way, and in knowing first that Christ is like a mother, I know now that He is there in every good thing that comes into my life and in every good person who offers a helping hand. He is all around us. Though none of us is THE Savior, all of us can participate in saving.

I know my Savior because I know my mother . . . and I hope that one day, my children and others will know God and our Savior Jesus Christ because they knew me and others who chose to "take up His cross" as we covenanted to do.

Jesus Christ *is* the Master Healer and our greatest source of relief. Sarah has come so far because of the healing power of the Savior and His Atonement as well as His working through others to provide relief. What a blessing it is that we can partner with the Master Healer to help bring emotional, spiritual, and physical relief to those around us.

Elder Dieter F. Uchtdorf said, "The Savior is the worker of miracles. He is the great Healer. He is our example, our light, even in the darkest moments."[19]

And Elder Neil L. Andersen added, "The Savior is our Good Samaritan, sent 'to heal the brokenhearted.' He comes to us when others pass us by. With compassion, He places His healing balm on our wounds and binds them up. He carries us. He cares for us. He bids us, 'Come unto me . . . and I shall heal [you].'"[20]

Some of the most beautiful and healing words from and about the Savior are found in the book of Isaiah, and they have often provided me with much-needed spiritual and emotional relief:

"When thou passest through the waters, I will be with thee; . . . when thou walkest through the fire, thou shalt not be burned . . . For I am the Lord thy God . . . thy Saviour . . . Thou [art] precious in my sight" (Isaiah 43:2–4).

"Fear thou not; for I am with thee: be not dismayed; for I am thy God: I will strengthen thee; yea, I will help thee; yea, I will uphold thee with the right hand of my righteousness" (Isaiah 41:10).

"Hast thou not heard, that the everlasting God . . . giveth power to the faint; and to them that have no might, he increaseth strength. . . . They that wait upon the Lord shall . . . mount up with wings as eagles" (Isaiah 40:28–29, 31).

"[I am come] to comfort all that mourn . . . to give unto them beauty for ashes, the oil of joy for mourning, the garment of praise for the spirit of heaviness" (Isaiah 61:2–3).

I witness from my own personal experience that Jesus Christ is our ultimate source of relief. He knows each one of us intimately, He loves each one of us dearly, and He desires to be a part of our lives and bless us with the divine relief we each so desperately need. I witness of His power and ability to strengthen us and give us that needed relief in His own time and in His own way, which will be the precise time and way He knows is best for each of us as we go through this learning and growing experience of mortality that will enable us to become like Him and return home to our Heavenly Parents. I witness that He lives. He *is* the Master Healer. Jesus Christ *is* relief.

Camille N. Johnson: Jesus Christ is the Master Healer, and He can lighten the burden of our physical and emotional ailments. This relief He provides—sometimes through others—is both spiritual and temporal. I want to expand upon the temporal relief the Savior offers to us and through us. Service—providing temporal relief—changes our natures and prepares us for the temple.

The Relief Society was organized to help prepare a people for the temple, both spiritually and temporally. Consistent with our original charge, today we continue to address the temporal needs of Heavenly Father's children all around the globe.

I recently had the opportunity to travel to the northeast corner of Uganda, an area known as Karamoja. It is part of the broader Horn of Africa, stricken by years of drought. There, women venture to a well—typically a thirty-minute walk each way—to carry all the water their family will need for the day. They are also constantly gathering firewood and charcoal. They are tending to chickens if they are fortunate enough to have them. The women birth babies and nurse babies and—day after day—work to find or trade for food to feed their families. The labor required to live there is monumental.

It was the first time I had personally seen such dire physical circumstances. And yet, I felt hope. The Church partnered with UNICEF to provide outreach, education, food and RUTFs (Ready to Use Therapeutic Food) for children who were severely malnourished, and the temporal relief we brought in the name of the Savior's Church brought hope to the most vulnerable of Heavenly Father's children.

Much of the outreach and education happened under a tree as women came together to learn what to eat when they are pregnant, how to screen children for malnutrition, and how to safely prepare nutritious food. They were tested for malaria and provided with mosquito nets. And they loved being together! Through a system much like ministering, the women then took what they had learned and shared it with others.

In Karamoja, I had a most profound manifestation of the love that our Heavenly Father and Savior have for the people there— each of them—and for each of us. The Good Shepherd's flock is known and numbered. He knows His children.

I hope that those women and children felt the love of God. We danced and sang together, and through an interpreter I had the opportunity to talk with them. "You must wonder why we are here," I said. "We are here and want to help because you are our sisters and brothers. We are all children of a loving Heavenly Father."

It is both a blessing and a covenantal responsibility for us to provide temporal relief to our sisters and brothers around the world.

My counselors and I have the privilege of working with the presiding bishopric in addressing the welfare needs of our members and the global community. We serve on the Welfare and Self-Reliance Executive Committee, which oversees thousands of welfare projects every year. As reflected in the Annual Report for 2022, the Church sponsored 3,692 humanitarian projects in 190 countries with expenditures totaling more than $1 billion. Church members and our friends donated 6.3 million hours of volunteer work.[21] The global effort of which we are a part is an extraordinary occasion, a pressing call, just as Emma anticipated!

There are legions who mourn, many in need of comfort, countless who are weak, hands hanging down with knees that are feeble.[22] The need is significant, and I testify that it is important. The Shepherd is relying upon us to tend to the needs of His sheep.

Like the caregivers of the man with palsy who brought him to the Savior,[23] it is important that we be the conduit through which the Savior provides temporal relief in our own communities. There is housing insecurity, food insecurity, emotional distress, pain, grief, lack of education, and disappointment in our own backyards, wherever we live.

Sometimes I think it is easier to provide temporal relief to people we do not know. Do we prefer to send food to distant countries or shoes to orphanages far away, imagining in our minds how joyfully our donations will be received? Those are noble efforts that can and should be accomplished as we make humanitarian donations to the Church. But what about the disagreeable lady who lives around the corner from you? Does she need relief? Perhaps the best humanitarian outreach is to reach across the fence or across the street.

We often hear the phrases, "lift where you stand"[24] or "bloom where you are planted."[25] What that means is that God puts you in a position to be a conduit through which He provides relief if you are willing. And when you provide relief to others, I testify that you will find the source of relief. You will find Jesus Christ.

It is our covenantal blessing to partner with Jesus Christ in providing relief, both temporal and spiritual, to all of God's children. Let us commit to being the conduit through which He provides relief. I know that in doing so we will find His relief, personally, and be blessed by the peaceful reassurance that we are never alone.

NOTES

1. "Nauvoo Relief Society Minute Book: March 17, 1842," www.church historianspress.org.
2. The Joseph Smith Papers, "Nauvoo Relief Society Minute Book," pg. 12, www.josephsmithpapers.org.
3. Emma Hale Smith, "We Are Going to Do Something Extraordinary," 1842–1844, www.churchhistorianpress.org.
4. See Gospel Topics, "Relief Society," Gospel Library.
5. Dallin H. Oaks, "The Keys and Authority of the Priesthood," *Ensign* or *Liahona*, May 2014.
6. Russell M. Nelson, "The Everlasting Covenant," *Liahona*, October 2022.
7. See 3 Nephi 19:23.
8. See Alma 37:37.
9. Russell M. Nelson, "Overcome the World and Find Rest," *Liahona*, November 2022.
10. Dale G. Renlund, "Accessing God's Power Through Covenants," *Liahona*, May 2023.
11. See Russell M. Nelson, "Sisters' Participation in the Gathering of Israel," *Ensign or Liahona*, November 2018.
12. See 3 Nephi 19:23.

13. Gordon B. Hinckley, "In the Arms of His Love," *Ensign*, November 2006.

14. See John 4:3–42.

15. James E. Faust, "The Light in Their Eyes," *Ensign* or *Liahona*, November 2005. Brigham Young's quote comes from his Office Journal, Jan. 28, 1857.

16. See Study Helps, "Forsake, Forsaken," Index to the Triple Combination, Gospel Library.

17. Camille N. Johnson, "Jesus Christ Is Relief," *Liahona*, May 2023.

18. Russell M. Nelson, "Why have faith now? LDS President Russell M. Nelson explains during Phoenix-area visit," *Arizona Republic*, Feb. 10, 2019, https://www.azcentral.com/story/opinion/op-ed/2019/02/10/viewpoints-lds-leader-urges-spirituality-secular-world-visits-phoenix-area/2776270002/.

19. Dieter F. Uchtdorf, "Four Titles," *Ensign* or *Liahona*, May 2013.

20. Neil L. Andersen, "Wounded," *Ensign* or *Liahona*, November 2018.

21. Newsroom, "The 2022 Report of How the Church of Jesus Christ Cared for Those in Need," 22 March 2023.

22. See Doctrine and Covenants 81:5.

23. See Mark 2:1-5.

24. Dieter F. Uchtdorf, "Lift Where You Stand," *Ensign* or *Liahona*, November 2008.

25. Video Collections, "Stand Ye in Holy Places—Bloom Where You're Planted," 2021 Doctrine and Covenants Media Resources.

BELIEVEST THOU THIS?

Lita Little Giddins

Dogs are known to be faithful, loyal, dependable, protective, courageous, affectionate, gentle, patient, intelligent, adaptable, loving, and helpful.

Do any of these characteristics describe your furry family members? Our regal, eighth furry family member is named Princess Winifred Giddins. She is going on fifteen years old and fits *all* of these characteristics. Our family would not be complete without our Winnie.

In the October 2022 General Conference, Sister J. Anette Dennis retold the story of a dog named Cassie and her owner, Jack. Jack had some expectations of Cassie; he wanted to show off how skilled she was to his friends. Those expectations went unmet and Jack became frustrated and angry. Cassie did not obey. Cassie let Jack down.

But why? What was going on with Jack's loyal, adaptable, dependable, and loving companion? Well, Jack discovered that

Cassie was injured quite seriously with deep wounds that went to the bone. The questions I had when reading this were:

- With injuries so serious, why was Jack unable to see them?
- What causes us to lose our ability to see and discern what is the "true character" of each other?
- And finally, are *we* the ones acting out of our "true character" at times?

If we *are* acting out of our "true character," why do we do that? One possible answer is the burden we carry from self-judgment. We are commanded to love God and our neighbors, that is true. But loving ourselves is also a part of the call to love, and most often, that is one of the most difficult commandments to obey (Luke 10:27).

Before I continue, let me define the word "judge" for our shared understanding. One definition is "to form an estimate or evaluation of"[1] someone or something. This definition tends to lean more toward our mortal perspectives. I experienced this type of judgment as a little girl.

When I was in fifth grade, my family lived in southern California, and I had a best friend named Becky. Becky and I loved playing together and she lived across the street from the elementary school we attended. Every day, we would meet at the corner, cross the street, and enter the school grounds together. One day, Becky was not there to meet me at the corner, so I decided to go to her house to pick her up. I knocked on the door. Her father opened it. With a big smile on my face I asked, "Is

Becky here? I'm her friend from school." Her father looked at me and said, "Becky's not going to school today." He shut the door. The next time I met up with Becky, she delivered the sad news. Becky told me her dad didn't want her to be my friend anymore because I was Black. That was my first major, heartbreaking experience of being judged by man because of the color of my skin. It is a painful memory to this very day.

The Guide to the Scriptures defines "to judge" this way: "to evaluate behavior in relation to the principles of the gospel; to decide; to discern good from evil."[2] I believe this is a more Christ-centered approach. But that doesn't mean it is easy.

The Lord has promised us, "For my yoke is easy and my burden is light" (Matthew 11:30). Because of the Atonement of Jesus Christ, I have come to hear the Savior's trusting assurance this way when it comes to judging: "For my yoke [His Atonement] is easy [discernable and accessible] and my burden [His ability to distinguish anything we carry, which He has the power and full capacity to consider accurately] is light." So to all who self-judge or feel judged, we are invited to take this "yoke" of grace, mercy, and compassion upon us, and learn of Him.

Sister Dennis continued her talk by quoting Elder Gary E. Stevenson, who explained, "When we confront life's wind and rainstorms, sickness and injuries, the Lord—our Shepherd, our Caregiver—will nourish us with love and kindness. He will heal our hearts and restore our souls."[3] What a beautiful promise! But there is another question to consider: *why*? Why will the Lord do this for us? Because He knows what it feels like to be judged and misjudged. Here are just a few scriptural witnesses:

- "And it came to pass that the angel spake unto me again, saying: Look! And I looked and beheld the Lamb of God, that he was taken by the people; yea, the Son of the everlasting God was judged of the world" (1 Nephi 11:32–33).
- "I came unto my own, and my own received me not" (3 Nephi 9:16).
- "And when he is come, he will reprove the world of sin, and of righteousness, and of judgment: . . . Of judgment, because the prince of this world is judged" (John 16:8, 11).
- "[Caiaphas said] . . . tell us whether thou be the Christ, the Son of God. Jesus saith unto him . . . Hereafter shall ye see the Son of man sitting on the right hand of power, and coming in the clouds of heaven. . . . [False witnesses said] He is guilty of death" (Matthew 26:63–64, 66).

Jesus of Nazareth was judged because of where He came from—a place where people were looked down upon and despised. Jesus of Nazareth was judged because of how He looked. Jesus of Nazareth was judged because of who He said *He* was. Jesus of Nazareth was judged because of what He did. For these reasons, and more, I believe His bowels were and are full of compassion for us because of what judgment means to Him.

Sister Dennis mentions the woman "caught in adultery" in the New Testament. To me, she is a woman who forgot whose she was. The crowd had passed judgment and was eager to condemn.

The Savior, however, extended a very self-reflective and merciful invitation: "He that is without sin among you, let him first cast a stone at her" (John 8:7).

Could it be that because He knew the thoughts and afflictions of the crowd and their many burdens, the Lord provided the opportunity for this woman's neighbors to self-reflect and draw from the well of mercy? Could it be that maybe the Lord knew judgment was pervasive among them, and this was an invitation to put down the metaphorical stones embedded in their hearts in order to see more clearly the healing that needed to occur within themselves and each other? Perhaps.

The queen of King Lamoni is an example of judgment from the Book of Mormon. Her husband, the king, had collapsed. Everyone judged him to be dead. But maybe we can learn a lesson about judging for ourselves from the queen who, beseeching Ammon, said, "Others say that he is dead and that he stinketh, and that he ought to be placed in the sepulchre; but as for myself, to me he doth not stink" (Alma 19:5).

How many of us have been in situations where we have misheard, seen inaccurately, misspoke, or regretted doing something based on an impulsive, emotional reaction? How can we learn to pause before judging and find ways to show love, the Christ-centered approach, instead?

Each one of us is trying to navigate through pains, difficulties, and uncertainties. We wonder what we need to hold onto to sustain life, and what we need to let go of. We wonder what to do to get out of our heads so that our hearts can take over. During such times, we might feel anxiety, fear, frustration, confusion, and doubt. So often the judgments we make are "reactions" to our lived experiences, our traumas, our assumptions, and our unmet expectations—like Jack's unmet expectations for Cassie. When we find ourselves casting judgment during these heavy and vulnerable times, when feelings escalate and manifest in our behavior, how do we respond?

Because we have the power to choose our actions, I invite you to take a step back and turn your attention to your breathing before becoming reactive in those heavy and vulnerable moments. Sometimes you might need to remove yourself from a situation to create some distance to process your thoughts and to seek a space where the Spirit can teach you how to respond to what you *think* you have seen, heard, or experienced. Remember the importance of distance as taught by Elder Rafael E. Pino in general conference: "Perspective is the way we see things when we look at them from a certain distance, and it allows us to appreciate their true value."[4]

Recently, I was in a sealing room doing the work of family members. While looking in the mirror and reflecting on our progression toward eternity, an impression came to me. It was this: Though we see far in the temple's repeating mirrors, we can't see everything. At a certain point, we cannot see any further. Likewise, our perspective is limited when it comes to our judgment of ourselves and others, even in the way we judge the Lord. The message from the temple mirrors is a reminder that we must trust Him, the One who knows what we can't know, who sees what we can't see, who judges each child of God completely and perfectly. He has an eternal perspective and is fully entrusted to appreciate our true value.

Let's return to the account of Ammon and the queen of King Lamoni for further insights regarding perspective.

When the queen testifies that, to her, the king does not smell, she communicates an alternate perspective at this pivotal moment: one of hope, an openness to the possibility that there is something more important to gain from this situation than what was anticipated.

Ammon explains to her, "He is not dead, but he sleepeth in God, and on the morrow he shall rise again." Ammon then asks, "Believest thou this?" (Alma 19:8–9).

What was Ammon attempting to help the queen have faith in and understand? That God was involved! To encourage her to see His hand in the situation. To not write her husband (and I will add, anyone) off by judging hastily, prematurely, or incorrectly. To remind her that the sun would rise the next day and bring a newness of hope and life. Wonderful people, do *you* believe this?

In the case of the queen, she believed in that newness of life right away! In awe Ammon exclaimed, "There has not been such great faith among all the people of the Nephites" (Alma 19:10).

What happened next? When King Lamoni arose the next day, the Spirit of the Lord was poured out upon him, his wife, and Ammon, who became overpowered with joy to witness that, despite the error of their ways, the Lord did not judge his brethren to condemnation. The Spirit had such an effect on that household that even the king's servants fell to the earth (see Alma 19:16).

Now, at the scene was a woman named Abish. She had kept her conversion a secret for many years, waiting for the day and time when incorrect, longstanding traditions would be righted. Why did she keep her conversion a secret? Possibly she feared the judgment of man (see Alma 19:17).

The story continues with the community of neighbors assembling to see their king and queen and everyone around them unconscious on the ground. Their gazes fall upon Ammon—a Nephite. The judgment begins. Here is what happens:

1. Some determine that it was the Nephite who caused the "evil" scene before them. One man seeking revenge for Ammon's earlier encounter with his brother attempts to kill Ammon but falls dead (see Alma 19:19–22).

2. People marvel and fear this great "power" and begin to contend among themselves. Some judge Ammon to be an instrument for good. Others objectify and label him not as human but as a "monster" (see Alma 19:26–27).

We all occasionally misjudge, like the people in this story. But Mormon counsels us to "take heed . . . that [we] do not judge that which is evil to be of God, or that which is good and of God to be of the devil" (Moroni 7:14).

In the story of Jack and Cassie, there was a moment in which Jack did not see Cassie as a loving, loyal companion. He saw her as an object of humiliation and embarrassment, which added to his woundedness on a mental, emotional, and spiritual level. Abish, similarly, must have been disappointed and upset by how her people were reacting to what she knew to be the power of God.

What we learn at this crucial juncture is that, though she may have had reason to feel anger, there was no contention in Abish. She exemplified President Russell M. Nelson's caution to avoid contention: "I am greatly concerned that so many people seem to believe that it is completely acceptable to condemn, malign, and vilify *anyone* who does not agree with them. . . . Anger never persuades. Hostility builds no one. Contention never leads to inspired solutions."[5]

Because Abish did not have a spirit of contention, *she* came up with an inspired solution to the problems she faced. Out of pure love and by human touch, she connected personally with the queen to lift her up. Then the queen humbly followed the example of this loyal member of her kingdom and lifted up her husband (see Alma 19:29–30).

President Nelson's message continued, "As disciples of Jesus Christ, we are to be examples of how to interact with others— *especially* when we have differences of opinion. One of the easiest ways to identify a *true follower* of Jesus Christ is how compassionately that person treats other people."[6]

Thank you, Abish, for such a beautiful example of how disciples of Jesus Christ interact with their sisters and brothers.

After being raised to new life, King Lamoni and Ammon taught the people. Despite the animosity sustained traditionally among them, human judgment was able to turn to Christ-centered judgment. For they *all* declared "that their hearts had been changed; that they had no more desire to do evil" (Alma 19:33).

From that miraculous launch point, we land at this testimony: "And thus the work of the Lord did commence among the Lamanites; thus the Lord did begin to pour out his Spirit upon them; and we see that his arm is extended to all people who will repent and believe on his name" (Alma 19:36).

And that's the happy ending of the story about judgment and perspective from the Book of Mormon. God is always good, y'all!

So where do we go from here? Let's take a final look at how the story of Jack and Cassie relates to our treatment of each other and wrap it all up in Jesus to get our answer. Jesus is wrapped up in everything.

Because the characteristics I listed at the beginning that describe our furry family members are also some of the characteristics of our forever eternal friend, Jesus Christ, I see Cassie as a symbol of Christ. Like Cassie, our Savior is known to be faithful, loyal, dependable, protective, courageous, affectionate, gentle, and patient. He assists, He is adaptable, He is loving.

Jesus knows of our burdens—the wounds and gashes in our minds, in our hearts, and in our spirits. Like Cassie, *He* was wounded to the bone that He might be able to come to our side to lovingly assist in our woundedness. It is *He* who should guide our impulses and our responses in every circumstance. When we take a step back to create distance for perspective, we allow *Him* to enter in. For He has promised, "I will not leave you comfortless" (John 14:18). This is a reassurance to me. I can imagine Him saying, "I am personally and intimately acquainted with your pain. So, *I* will help you through *your* healing, *your* growing, *your* need to see."

And what does our Savior want to help us see? That we *all* are literal children of Heavenly Parents. Our divine identity is important, but I also believe it is His desire to help us see *the literal child* in each other. This has become my heartfelt prayer:

"Father in Heaven, it's me. Thy daughter, Lita. Please, teach me how to see the literal child in my sisters and brothers—in the person standing in front of or sitting right next to me. Please, teach me how to see their wounds and their noble and divine characteristics. To resist the temptation to see something 'less' in them instead of everything that is 'more' about them, and to take a step back so I can create the space I need in order to see it. Please, reframe my thoughts and reposition my heart that I may think more like Thee and love more freely, more completely, like Thee."

Maybe Becky would still be my friend if her dad had offered a similar prayer and seen me this way.

Once Jack took a step back and removed himself from that charged space of frustration, embarrassment, and anger, his perspective changed from man's judgment to Christ-centered judgment. When that happened, he found himself in shock at the state he found Cassie in. It is here that I believe the story invites us to see ourselves as Jack in terms of our relationship with Christ and our discipleship.

Jack came to understand the sacrifice, the suffering, and the source of the wounds on this symbol of Christ. And when he gained that personal witness, he took his loyal, protective, dependable, loving friend into his arms, and the little boy in him began to weep with a purer heart of profound gratitude and love. His character became more Christlike.

I add my voice to Nephi's testimony of the Savior's miraculous atoning sacrifice: "O the greatness of the mercy of our God. . . . he suffereth the pains of . . . every living creature, both men, women, and children" (2 Nephi 9:19, 21). I would continue by echoing the words in Helaman, "O remember . . . remember that there is no other way nor means whereby man can be saved, only through *the atoning blood* of Jesus Christ who shall come; yea . . . he cometh to redeem the world" (Helaman 5:9, emphasis added).

His yoke *is* easy. His burden *is* light. May this testimony ring true for each of us. For then, we *shall* find rest and we *will* have peace. Wonderful people, children of God, "Believest thou this?"[7]

NOTES

1. "judge." *Merriam-Webster.com*, 2023, https://www.merriam-webster.com.
2. Guide to the Scriptures, "Judge," scriptures. ChurchofJesusChrist.org.
3. Gary E. Stevenson, "Hearts Knit Together," *Liahona*, May 2021.
4. Rafael E. Pino, "The Eternal Perspective of the Gospel," *Ensign* or *Liahona*, May 2015.
5. Russell M. Nelson, "Peacemakers Needed," *Liahona*, May 2023.
6. Russell M. Nelson, "Peacemakers Needed," *Liahona*, May 2023.
7. Alma 19:9.

LOVING AND LIFTING OUR LGBTQ CHILDREN WITH CHRIST AS OUR GUIDE

Allison Dayton

Many families in The Church of Jesus Christ of Latter-day Saints, including my own, have a child that identifies as LGBTQ. With this identification come many heartfelt questions, concerns, and discussions as our child navigates their own decisions on their terms. Elder Quentin L. Cook challenges, "Let us be at the forefront in terms of expressing love, compassion, and outreach. . . . Let's not have families exclude or be disrespectful of those who choose a different lifestyle as a result of their feelings about their own gender [and/or orientation]."[1]

How do I have open conversations with love, respect, and support as I acknowledge the difficulties faced by my LGBTQ child? How does my personal covenant relationship with my Savior enhance my ability to walk with my child while they make decisions about their life? How do I partner with the Lord in supporting and loving my LGBTQ child? How can I help them build their own relationship with Christ and the assurance that they are loved as a child of God?

I have always been in an LGBTQ family. My oldest brother Preston is gay, and my son Jake is gay. Four years ago, I started an organization called Lift + Love to help support LGBTQ families. We work with thousands of individuals and family members like you. They come to church for the much-needed peace the gospel can bring only to be confronted with questions and tensions, both internal and external, that they could have never imagined. This tension creates immense pain and threatens the loss of connection to the gospel.

In my work, people always want to know how I stay active in the Church. I am going to be real with you: sometimes it's really hard. For me, it is about connection. After all, the gospel of Jesus Christ is, at its very foundation, about eternal connection. Staying closely connected to the Lord helps me navigate this journey. Staying close to my son helps me support him as he navigates his.

This past Christmas, my side of the family traveled to the Holy Land and Egypt for a once-in-a-lifetime trip. While there, we saw the pyramid at Giza, a vast building known for its triangular walls.

Did you know that the triangle is the strongest shape? I thought the square was, but if you put enough pressure on one side of a square it will collapse into a rhombus, just like the boxes in your basement. Even if big pressure is applied to one side of a triangle, the other sides will compress and stretch to absorb the tension, keeping the shape sure.

Because of its ability to take pressure, I think the triangle is a powerful shape to use when talking about three eternal connections that are critical to navigating this journey and how they work together. First, our connection to our children. Second, our connection to God. Third, our child's connection to God. I will also speak to two critically important support systems: family support and ward and stake leader support.

THE POWER OF ETERNAL CONNECTIONS

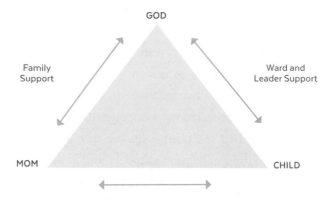

First Connection: Us to Our Children

Elder Jeffrey R. Holland said, "No love in mortality comes closer to approximating the pure love of Jesus Christ than the selfless love a devoted mother has for her child."[2]

My mom passed away about a year ago. Not long ago, I was going through paperwork and found a talk she had given at her stake women's conference in 1997. She told a story that happened in the 1970s, in a time when most parents lost connection with their gay children.

She began her talk,

> One lovely Sunday afternoon, Brooke and I were sitting with our family in sacrament meeting. The bishop was talking about his concern about many problems of the families in our ward. In fact, he said there were only three families that weren't dealing with a rather serious problem. Brooke and I smiled and wondered who the other two families were.
>
> Several weeks later, our whole world crumbled in an instant when we found out from our bishop that our oldest son—the wonderful, bright, outstanding boy we loved with all our hearts—was gay.

My mom's first thoughts came in a jumble: "Not our son, it couldn't be." "What did we do wrong?" "We tried to be such good parents." "We carefully raised him according to everything we knew was right." "How could we make him better?" "How could we make him change to be 'normal?'"

She continued,

> As we sought help for him and for our family and struggled with our feelings of anger, guilt, denial and fear we went through a difficult journey of understanding. Over the years we have come face-to-face with the power of love and we know that God does not abandon us.
>
> We have found we had an enormous capacity to love as

we have reconciled our feelings about a society that misunderstands him, a religion that rejects him, and a God who loves him.

My life has been enriched by having a gay son. And I will support him every step of the way.

To speak openly about having a gay son twenty-six years ago was likely the bravest public thing my mom ever did.

My parents fully loved and supported Preston. He was an important part of our family, and so was his partner. But my brother came out to the world in the 1980s, when the world thought being gay was a choice. He was called a deviant. He was blamed for not being faithful enough to cure himself. He constantly heard the message that there was something terribly, terribly wrong with him.

These messages damaged him. They disconnected him from himself, from the Church, and from his identity as a child of God. His life was full of pain. Six years ago, at the age of fifty-eight, my brother Preston ended his own life. His last words describe an unbearable sadness that he was not accepted, or acceptable, as he was.

Preston's death and his pain were particularly hard because I had received clear spiritual promptings that my own son Jake was gay. A year later, Jake came into our room late at night, shut the door, and said we needed to talk.

Gratefully, because of my brother, we were prepared for this moment. When he said the words, "I'm gay," we were ready with the love and support we knew he needed. We pulled our big eighteen-year-old boy in between us on our bed and told him how much we loved him and that we knew how much God loved him. That sacred moment was one of absolute peace for all three of us—so peaceful that my husband fell asleep while we were talking.

Jake graduated from BYU last year and is off at grad school. He has a lot of difficult choices ahead of him, choices that only he can make, but we know he's thoughtful, and he will be guided by the Spirit. And he has us, and we will support him *every step of the way*!

The Second Connection: Us to God

I've been wrestling with the complexities of this space for forty years. Sometimes this process has been exquisitely painful. I've worried I'd lose faith in the Church or in God. I've cycled through confusion and fear and there are times when I have come to the Savior with *red hot* anger and open wounds.

I've tested the Savior's promise in James 1, the very scripture that Joseph Smith turned to when he had questions: "If any of you lack wisdom, let him ask of God" (James 1:5).

We all know the King James Version, but I'm going to share these verses with you from the New International Version because the wording is a little more modern and conversational.

Consider it pure joy, my brothers and sisters, whenever you face trials of many kinds, because you know that the testing of your faith produces perseverance. Let perseverance finish its work so that you may be mature and complete, not lacking anything. If any of you lacks wisdom, you should ask God, who gives generously to all without finding fault, and it will be given to you. (James 1:2–5, New International Version)

Testing this pattern has given me confidence to go to the Lord with every bit of anger, frustration, and all the questions I might have. And I have a lot of questions.

About a month before my son came out, he wasn't doing very well. He was hurting and angry. I felt like he was disappearing into himself, and he'd all but stopped talking. We had an honest, real conversation about depression and suicide and asked some questions from an online test; he self-scored high on half of them. The next morning, I called a therapist and his pediatrician and got help.

Watching Jake struggle against himself was breaking my heart and breaking me down. It had barely been a year since my brother's death; I wasn't going to let the same thing happen to my son.

Later that morning, somehow, I dragged myself to a book club lunch that I didn't want to go to. I was trying to keep it together when my daughter texted me a photo. She was on a BYU study abroad for her major in Copenhagen, Denmark, at the church where the original marble Christus sits, and she'd sent me a picture of it. The photo of Christ with His hands reaching forward filled my broken heart with such sweet peace.

As I was looking at it, I realized there was an inscription under the feet of the Savior. It said "KOMMER TIL MIG." I happened to be sitting across the table from a dear friend who served her mission in Denmark, so I asked her, "What does this mean?"

With her big, warm smile, she said, "It means *come to me*."

So easy: just come to Me.

That's my how—I go to Him.

And rather than rebuke in times of pain, *He* gives me peace that I can hold onto until pain subsides. The peace He sends usually comes from others, like my friend who happened to speak Danish, and from the many others who love, minister to, and support our family. I have been the recipient of goodness from countless inspired women who have lifted me up and bound my wounds.

Even with these tender mercies, it is not easy for LGBTQ families to come to Him in the ways we had so easily before. So, we must find new ways to deepen our connection to God so we can go to Him.

Scriptures have been a critical tool for living in this tension. As I read with all the questions I have as a mother, the Spirit teaches me in new ways.

I read about Eve, who was faced with a complicated choice she had to make for the good of her family. Because of her wisdom and strength, she grew in understanding and reliance on God.[3]

Jochebed put her baby Moses in a basket and sent him down the river, knowing he would probably be raised outside of her faith. She trusted that God would protect and guide him.[4] I see the same faith in many families whose LGBTQ children are leaving or have left the Church.

Notice how often women and mothers in scripture partner with God to solve complicated problems. Eve, Jochebed, Rebekah,[5] Esther,[6] Sariah,[7] Mary,[8] Elizabeth,[9] Abish,[10] and more, all were guided to a solution different than the norms of their day.

Notice there are no perfect families in the scriptures. *Not one.*

But there are plenty of families in complicated situations. And when they turn to the Savior, He guides them. In each story, He says, "I know you feel broken or forgotten, but watch what happens with your faith and My power."

Another tool I've relied on is the temple. Recently, I felt a nudge to serve as an ordinance worker in the temple.

The initiatory ordinances[11] are a reminder of the power of God's blessings that I have access to as I strive to be faithful. These blessings include an increase of strength, an ability to know truth from error, protection from the adversary, and a reminder that we are to have *joy* in our families—even when they are imperfect. Maybe because they are imperfect.

In the endowment,[12] I've learned the importance the Lord places on agency. We are meant to learn by our own bitter and sweet experiences. We're promised further light and knowledge as we *ask*, *seek*, and *knock*.[13] He wants us to ask. He is anxious to teach us. And for me, the endowment has been a place of important personal revelation about my unique family and the plan the Lord has for each of us.

These are some of my tools for navigating the tension in this journey. They aren't going to fit everyone. Regardless of the tools you use, I believe what President Nelson testified in the April 2023 General Conference. Whatever the question or problem, "the answer is always found in the life and teachings of Jesus Christ."[14]

I invite you to go to Him. Trust Him. As you do you will know the power of His eternal connection. *Trust* Him to guide you. He is the way.

Third Connection: Your Child to God

Brace yourself: this is the hard part. Notice we parents are nowhere in this connection.

I know we love these babies, and we want to march them right to their full potential. But we also know it's not the Lord's way. Many of our children will use their agency and make decisions that drive us crazy or cause big heartaches. This experience is hardly limited to our LGBTQ children.

Have faith, not fear. The Savior is the connection. Our children are His children. He knows them, and He will guide them in ways that they understand. The best thing we can do is teach them young and remind them often that His hands are always stretched out as He says, "Come unto me" (Matthew 11:28 and Ether 12:27).

If you have lost connection with LGBTQ loved ones, do what you can to reconnect. They desperately need us to stay connected and supportive. Our LGBTQ children are under attack. The voices of the world tell them they are not valued as they are. The voices say they are not divine children of God. The voices of the world tell them that there is something terribly, terribly wrong with them.

Our children are constantly hearing these dangerous messages that cause shame and separation (spiritually and emotionally) from themselves, from family, and from God.

Even after all we can do, many of us will watch our children walk away from the Church. Or from us. If this happens, you may have to change the way you connect a little. We know the gospel can be a feast for the soul, but it can never be enjoyed if it's force-fed. Find common ground to rebuild your relationship.

When the fear creeps in, and I know it does, remember what Joseph Smith taught the women in the very first days of the Relief Society: "If you live up to your privilege, the angels cannot be restrained from being your associates."[15]

Mothers, go to the Savior and ask for his angels to watch over your child. Have faith. *You* are in divine partnership with Heaven. As we protect and nurture our relationships with our children, we will be a powerful tether stretching between our children and the Savior.

There are two important supportive factors I want to touch on that can make large differences in our LGBTQ children's overall well-being.

Support from Family

Studies, including the "Family Acceptance Project,"[16] which was created with a Latter-day Saint researcher, show that LGBTQ children who are highly rejected by their parents—meaning they are kicked out, blamed, told they can't talk about their orientation, or told their orientation is against God—are "8.4 times more likely to report having attempted suicide, 5.9 times more likely to report high levels of depression, and 3.4 times more likely to use illegal drugs"[17] when compared with LGBTQ youth who are not at all, or only slightly, rejected by their parents.

These are shocking numbers that prove that the family is

vitally important not only for the spiritual health of our LGBTQ children, but for their good mental health and well-being.

Tom Christofferson tells a story about his LGBTQ family in his book, *That We May Be One: A Gay Mormon's Perspective on Faith and Family*.[18] Years ago, his family was going on vacation, and Tom wanted to bring his partner. One of the brothers was so uncomfortable with this that he thought he might not bring his children on the trip. His mom and dad gathered his four brothers and his sisters-in-law for a council.

Tom remembers, "They began with prayer, and then, as I recall, my father talked about the importance of unity and loyalty to one another. My mother said, 'I am ashamed to say it, but there was a time when I thought we were the perfect Mormon family . . . but then life happens, and I realized that there is no perfect Mormon family. The only thing we can really be perfect at is loving each other.'"

His mother continued, "The most important lesson your children will learn from how our family treats their Uncle Tom is that nothing they can ever do will take them outside the circle of our family's love."

Tom said that became their guiding principle.[19]

When we realize the goal is not to have a perfect Latter-day Saint family but to become perfect at loving one another, we can grow together and become stronger as we partner with each other and the Lord.

Support from Wards and Leaders

It's been fifty years since my parents realized my brother was gay, and in many ways, we are in a vastly different world.

We know now that being LGBTQ is not a choice. Because our children are so young and vulnerable, many parents are fiercely protective of their emotional, physical, and spiritual well-being. These messages no longer land on the individual alone. They are felt by and threaten to disconnect the entire family, often before local leaders know that there is an LGBTQ person in the family.

The latest Gallup research says 7.1 percent of adults identify as LGBTQ.[20] That means if your ward has 300 people, 21 people in your ward might identify somewhere on the LGBTQ spectrum. That is a big number and it doesn't include their family members, who are also affected by both positive and negative messaging.

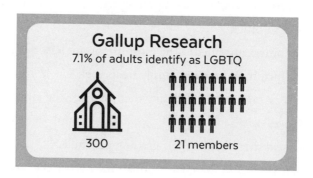

Local leaders and ward members play such a vital connective role in helping individuals and families know that they belong.

Most people I meet are desperately trying to stay connected. Jean B. Bingham, former Relief Society General President, talked about this kind of disconnection during the BYU Women's Conference in 2021. She taught,

> Studies have shown that the number one reason people leave religion is that they feel judged or unwelcome. That is cited more often than doctrinal disagreement or lack of belief. The good news is that situation can practically be eliminated if we really open our arms and hearts to everyone. We can seek to "be a light, not a judge." That is something left only to the Lord. Our responsibility is to extend an open hand and heart. As we do that, we find that we have created a safe place for sharing, a safe place to grow, a safe place to become our best selves.[21]

Get to know the resources for LGBTQ members on the church website.[22] There is good information for families and leaders there, including Elder Cook's challenge to us all: "As a church, nobody should be more loving and compassionate. Let us be at the forefront of expressing love, compassion, and outreach."[23]

President Nelson has often spoken of the gathering of Israel. In general conference, he has said, "The Savior's message is clear: His true disciples build, lift, encourage, persuade, and inspire—no matter how difficult the situation. True disciples of Jesus Christ are peacemakers."

He continued, "My dear brothers and sisters, the best is yet to come for those who spend their lives building up others. Today I invite you to examine your discipleship within the context of the way you treat others. I bless you to make any adjustments that may be needed so that your behavior is ennobling, respectful, and representative of a true follower of Jesus Christ."[24]

We are called to be gatherers, connectors. Our heavenly parents' LGBTQ children and their families need our open hands and open hearts to help them stay connected and close so they can feel the light and warmth of the Savior's gospel.

My testimony of the Savior has been forged along this journey. I count it all joy that I was raised in a loving, faithful LGBTQ family. I have been stretched. I have had to dig in. Because I've had to rely on the Savior, I have come to know Him, and I know I am known by Him. He strengthens and guides me. I testify that the Lord *loves* His LGBTQ children exactly as they are, and I believe they have much to teach us.

NOTES

1. Quentin L. Cook, "How Can I Include or Reach Out to Those Who Experience Same-Sex Attraction in My Ward or Stake?" *Life Help: Same Sex Attraction*, Gospel Library.
2. Jeffrey R. Holland, "Behold Thy Mother," *Ensign* or *Liahona*, November 2015.
3. See Genesis 3.
4. See Exodus 2:1–4.
5. See Genesis 22–49.
6. See the book of Esther.
7. See 1 Nephi 1.
8. See Study Helps: Guide to the Scriptures, "Mary, Mother of Jesus," Gospel Library.
9. See Luke 1.

10. See Alma 19.

11. See "Prophetic Teachings on Temples," *Endowment Initiatory-Washing and Anointing*, Gospel Library.

12. See "Prophetic Teachings on Temples," *Endowment Overview*, Gospel Library.

13. See Matthew 7:7.

14. Russell M. Nelson, "The Answer Is Always Jesus Christ," *Liahona*, May 2023.

15. *Relief Society Minute Book*, Nauvoo, Illinois, Apr. 28, 1842, Church History Library, 38.

16. San Francisco State University, "Welcome to the Family Acceptance Project, "https://familyproject.sfsu.edu/.

17. C. Ryan, "Engaging families to support lesbian, gay, bisexual and transgender (LGBT) youth: The Family Acceptance Project," *The Prevention Researcher* (2010), 11–13.

18. Tom Christofferson, *That We May Be One: A Gay Mormon's Perspective on Faith and Family*, 2017.

19. Candice Madsen, "Christofferson Brothers Share How They Remained 'As One,'" *KSL News*, October 2017. https://www.ksl.com/article /46175330/christofferson-brothers-share-how-they-remained-as-one.

20. Jeffery M. Jones, "LGBT Identification in U.S. Ticks Up to 7.1%," *Gallup News*, February 2022. https://news.gallup.com/poll/389792 /lgbt-identification-ticks-up.aspx.

21. "The Promise of Belonging," Jean B. Bingham, Sharon Eubank, and Reyna I. Aburto, BYU Women's Conference, April 2021.

22. https://site.churchofjesuschrist.org/study/life-help/same-sex-attraction ?lang=eng.

23. Quentin L. Cook, "How Can I Include or Reach Out to Those Who Experience Same-Sex Attraction in My Ward or Stake?" *Life Help: Same Sex Attraction*, Gospel Library.

24. Russell M. Nelson, "Peacemakers Needed," *Liahona*, May 2023.

OUR SAVIOR'S LOVE

Susan L. Gong

The change from "visiting teaching to ministering in a high and holier way"[1] invites us to think more deeply about the new commandment that the Savior gave his disciples: "As I have loved you, . . . love one another" (John 13:34). I want to share three observations about what it might mean to love as Jesus loves.

Understand

First, Jesus knows the heart of every child of God. In the New Testament, we see that he understands the essential nature of every person he meets. He knows Nathanael is a man without guile (see John 1:49). He knows Nicodemus, the Pharisee who comes to see Jesus in the middle of the night, is truly seeking to understand (see John 3:1–9). And from the beginning, He understands that Peter—impetuous, hopeful, vulnerable, two-steps-forward-one-step-back Peter—has it within him to lead the Church, or else why would Christ, on their very first meeting, give him the name Cephas, meaning "a stone" (John 1:42)?

Christ knows the heart of the Samaritan woman to whom He said, "Thou hast well said, I have no husband: for thou hast had five husbands; and he whom thou now hast is not thy husband" (John 4:17–18). Those words must have been spoken with incredible tenderness because they evoke such a humble response, perhaps one full of wonder: "Sir, I perceive that thou art a prophet" (John 4:19).

He knows the hearts of His persecutors, as demonstrated by His words: "Father, forgive them; for they know not what they do" (Luke 23:35).

There is healing and there is hope in just being known, just being understood. Perhaps you instinctively know the hearts of those you minister to. Perhaps you have that incredible gift of discernment. I do not. So if I am to love as Jesus would love, what do I need to do? I need to learn to listen.

When Elder Gong and I lived in Hong Kong, our apartment was located on one of the busiest streets in one of the busiest cities in the world. It was often hard to hear Gerrit unless we stood face-to-face.

One day Gerrit said in frustration, "Sweetheart, when we're next in Salt Lake, will you please have your hearing tested?" I obligingly visited an audiologist who, after testing my hearing, proclaimed, "Mrs. Gong, I have good news and bad news. The good news is your hearing is perfect. The bad news is that may

mean you have a listening problem, and there's not much I can
do about that."

So I am on notice: I need to learn to listen better. I need to
put down my electronic devices. I need to shut out the distractions and turn off the little voice in my head that's constantly
reminding me of all the things on my to-do list. And then I need
to listen with my heart to understand not just what someone is
saying, but who it is I'm talking to: a child of God. I'm discovering that listening means not just hearing the other person but
listening to the Holy Ghost as well. The Holy Ghost helps us ask
inspired questions that lead us to greater understanding.

Feel Compassion

A second observation from the scriptures about how Jesus
loves us is that compassion always accompanies Christ's understanding of our hearts. He has compassion on the blind,[2] on the
widow of Nain,[3] on lepers,[4] on the brother of Jared,[5] on one possessed with a devil,[6] and, multiple times, He has compassion on
the multitude.[7] From the cross, He voices compassion for Mary,
His mother.[8] Surely it is through His compassion that "he hath
borne our griefs" (Isaiah 53:4).

Compassion is at the heart of Christ's parables: The parable of
the debtor,[9] the story of the Good Samaritan,[10] and the father in
the parable of the prodigal son[11] all exhibit compassion.

For most of us, compassion requires imagination and intention. In our spheres of ministering, we can strive to understand
how it really feels

- to wrangle adorable and demanding preschoolers day in and day out.
- to be a divorced mom reentering the workforce after many years.
- to be 90 and alone.
- to be the returning prodigal.
- to have been abandoned or abused.
- to receive a diagnosis of cancer.
- to have been abused.
- to have lost a child to illness.
- to have lost a child to the world.

As Christians, we are called to feel the pain of others. In this we truly "bear one another's burdens" (Mosiah 18:8). When we have compassion—true empathy—something wondrous happens. We begin to know how to help.

Bless

This is my third observation about how Jesus loves: Having taken upon himself our infirmities, He knows how to succor us. Having felt our fear, our want, our loneliness, our hunger, our hurt, He responds to our specific need. He comforts, supplies, feeds, heals, nurtures, teaches, and blesses us.

Like the Good Samaritan, when Christ finds us suffering, He has compassion on us, He comes to us, binds our wounds, and brings us to the inn and cares for us (see Luke 10:33). The Church is the inn where we, like the innkeeper, are called upon to minister to each other until the Master returns.

Know the heart. Feel compassion. Bless. This is the Savior's pattern of ministering, and it can be ours.

I recently lost a dear friend who lived by this pattern. At her funeral, her daughter said, "My mother was good at everything important and special. She wanted everyone to have their story known. She paid notice in the most significant ways. How can you give up on yourself when your mom is this most profound person who sees you as you are and still believes in you?"

Another eulogy described this dear Christlike sister like this: "She was the giver of thoughtful gifts, the rescuer of stranded souls, a healer of broken hearts, a polisher of tarnished halos. She was the kind of person who always held the mirror at the most flattering angle. A woman of substance. She was observant of human need. Her response to suffering was always to ease the burden. Hers was love unfeigned."

As I hear the prophet call us to a higher, holier form of ministry, I think of my friend. We are being asked to love as she loved—to be good at what is special and important. But where do we get the patience, insight, imagination, courage, and strength to love like this?

A few years ago I had the blessing of attending the Salt Lake Temple with a recently endowed friend, a sister I've known since elementary school. Life has presented her with many challenges, and her connection with the Church has sometimes been tenuous, though I believe she has always had a spark of the gospel in her heart.

As we walked the corridors of that magnificent temple, she

stopped at every painting of the Savior, reached toward it, then bowed her head and touched her heart. In the celestial room she prayed fervently—having finally come to the house of the Lord, she was in no hurry to leave. On our way home, we walked through a bookstore, each of us browsing different sections.

Coming up behind me, she whispered, "Susan, you've got to see this! Someone has painted a picture of me!" We rounded a corner. She pointed to a beautiful image created by Brian Kershisnik featuring a woman surrounded by angels, all of whom were reaching out to help her.[12] "That's me!" my friend exclaimed. "That's just how I feel!"

Loved.

Blessed.

I testify that because we are loved with the "matchless bounty of the [Savior's] love" (Alma 26:15) and with the infinite love of our Heavenly Father, through Their love we can come to understand one another, have compassion for one another, and bless one another, in every way that is important and special. "We love him because he first loved us" (1 John 4:19). Because He loves us, we can learn to love and minister to one another. The Holy Ghost will help us know how.

NOTES

1. Sharon Eubank, "That We May All Sit Down in Heaven Together" May 3, 2018, BYU Women's Conference (Quoting President Russell M. Nelson, April 2018, General Authority Training).
2. See John 9:1–7.
3. See Luke 7:12; BD Burial 'widow of Nain.'
4. See Luke 17:12.

5. See Ether 3:6–13.
6. See Mark 5:1–13; Luke 4:33–37.
7. See 3 Nephi 17:7, 9; Matthew 9:36, Matthew 14:14, Matthew 15:32; Mark 8:2.
8. See John 19:27.
9. See Luke 7:41.
10. See Luke 10:30.
11. See Luke 15:11–32.
12. Brian Kershisnik, "She Will Find What Is Lost," used with permission.

FINDING YOUR PLACE IN THE UNIVERSE

Denise Stephens

ADAPTED FROM A BYU DEVOTIONAL

Years ago, my husband bought me a cute little plaque that says, "If it weren't for the last minute, I would never get anything done." I am sure we can all relate.

In our hurried and rushed lives, we often focus too much on the things that have deadlines, and we fail to make time for the things that matter most. We forget who we really are, and we lose sight of the eternal. We fail to take the time to pray, to ponder, to seek personal revelation, to follow the promptings of the Spirit, to recognize God's hand in our lives, and to feel His love. With eyes cast down and our focus on the task at hand, we forget to look up.

I want to remind all of us to take the time to look up.

All Things Bear Record of God

I am an astronomer, and I have always been fascinated with space. One of my earliest memories involves being at a school book fair when I was five or six years old and picking up a picture book containing photographs of Jupiter and its moons.

The *Voyager* spacecraft had just arrived at Jupiter and had returned the most stunning images of the four Galilean moons. I can still remember pictures of the moon Io in this book, with its volcanoes and intense orange and yellow colors. This little moon, just slightly larger than Earth's moon, should have been geologically dead—a gray, cratered world similar to our own moon. Instead, it presented a beautiful, chaotic, changing landscape that absolutely intrigued me as a child. I was hooked.

As an astronomer, I often wonder why God created objects like the moon Io? If you really think about it, there is no reason for our solar system to consist of anything more than a sun, a moon, and an earth. So why put eight planets around the sun instead of one? Why create exotic moons like Io around giant planets? Why create Pluto and his friends in the Kuiper belt?

As I have studied God's creations in the heavens, I have come to believe that all of God's creations serve a purpose and exist for a reason. When Moses asked God to tell him "why these things are so," God's response was, "For mine own purpose have I made these things. Here is wisdom and it remaineth in me" (Moses 1:30–31).

We may not know the whys of all of God's creations, but each of God's vast creations is a reminder that He is in charge, that there is a divine plan, and that we are here on this earth for a much greater purpose than what the world would espouse.

The Lord taught Adam:

And behold, all things have their likeness, and all things are created and made to bear record of me, both things which are temporal, and things which are spiritual; things which are in the heavens above, and things which are on the earth, and things which are in the earth, and things which are under the earth, both above and beneath: all things bear record of me. (Moses 6:63)

Likewise, Alma taught:

The scriptures are laid before thee, yea, and all things denote there is a God; yea, even the earth, and all things that are upon the face of it, yea, and its motion, yea, and also all the planets which move in their regular form do witness that there is a Supreme Creator. (Alma 30:44)

Each of God's creations is a witness that He lives.

God's Most Important Creation: You

Sadly, we have done our best to build concrete jungles and light-polluted skies that block our views of God's creations. We walk through this life with screens in front of our faces and plugs in our ears, completely oblivious to the wonder that surrounds us. With all of our technological advances, we have become complacent, like the Nephites. If you recall, after the sign of Christ's birth was given, Nephi recorded, "And it came to pass that . . . the people began to forget those signs and wonders which they had heard, and began to be less and less astonished at a sign or a wonder from heaven, insomuch that they began to be hard in their hearts, and blind in their minds, and began to disbelieve all which they had heard and seen" (3 Nephi 2:1).

When you look at a picture of a star-forming region like the Orion Nebula, do you realize how blessed you are to live in a day and age when the Lord has provided us with the technology to view His vast creations in the process of creation? Do you realize that only the prophets of old, such as Adam, Abraham, Enoch, and Moses, were blessed with the knowledge we have today—knowledge so great that it caused Moses to exclaim, "Now, for this cause I know that man is nothing, which thing I never had supposed" (Moses 1:10).

I want to challenge you to put the phones away and to put aside YouTube and video games and to take time each day to be a witness to creation. Take a walk and feel the breeze on your face, run your hand through the grass, enjoy a starry night sky, and give thanks for a Supreme Creator, who has made this world for you.

Heavenly Father loves you, and He knows you. Among all of His creations, you are the most important.

A Lesson from the Stars

Thanks to modern revelation, we know much about what happened in the premortal life, the purpose of this earth and our sojourn on it, and the exaltation that awaits us after this life if we are faithful. We also know something about the glory of stars.

In Abraham 3, the Lord gave Abraham an astronomy lesson. Abraham related, "And I saw the stars, that they were very great, and that one of them was nearest unto the throne of God; and there were many great ones which were near unto it; and the Lord said unto me: These are the governing ones; and the name of the great one is Kolob, because it is near unto me, for I am the Lord thy God: I have set this one to govern all those which belong to the same order as that upon which thou standest" (Abraham 3:2–3).

I am going to do my best to give you an astronomy lesson about the different glories of stars based on the limited knowledge of man.

When you look at stars in the night sky, they all appear to be roughly the same. That is because they are so far away. They appear as points of light, and they are so dim that not enough photons reach your eye for you to distinguish the color of most stars.

But if you look closely, you will notice that the brighter stars tend to be red or blue. Stars aren't all white. Their color corresponds to their temperature. And when you are able to calculate the distance to a star, you can determine its luminosity, or its true brightness. By combining information about the temperature and luminosity of a star, we can calculate its radius.

When we plot the luminosity of a star against its temperature, we get a plot called a Hertzsprung–Russell (H–R) diagram. What we have found is that stars are not all the same; they vary in glory.

Betelgeuse is one of the largest stars in our galaxy. It is colder than the sun, but it is much brighter and produces far more energy than the sun does. It is a supergiant star that is about 1,000 times larger in radius than the sun. If we replaced our sun with Betelgeuse, it would engulf all of the planets out to Jupiter!

Betelgeuse, along with other supergiant stars, is near the end of its life and will die soon—in the next fifty million years or so.

The smallest stars, called white dwarfs, are not really stars. A star is an object that produces energy through nuclear fusion; a white dwarf is the leftover core of a star that has died and shed its outer layers into space. In the Cat's Eye Nebula, there is a white dwarf at the center surrounded by layers of gas that were blown off when the star died. Seven billion years from now, when our sun dies, it may look very similar to this nebula, with a white dwarf at the center.

If you compare the glory of the sun to the other stars, it becomes quite obvious that the sun is not a great star. It is not the largest. It is not the hottest. And it is not the brightest. But even though it is not the greatest, the sun perfectly fills the measure of its creation. It provides the energy we need for life on this earth. If it were hotter or more luminous, it would be too hot for water to be a liquid on the surface of the earth, and life could not exist. And if the sun were colder or fainter, we would freeze.

As you further compare the sun's characteristics—such as its color, lifetime, and magnetic activity—to that of other stars, you quickly realize that stars like the sun are ideal for providing an environment that can sustain life. The sun has the perfect set of attributes to fulfill the calling it has been given.

After the Lord taught Abraham about the differences in stars, he began to teach Abraham about the intelligences or spirits that existed before this earth. Abraham saw you and me and all of the spirit children of God.

The Lord taught Abraham, "Howbeit that he made the greater star; as, also, if there be two spirits, and one shall be more intelligent than the other, yet these two spirits, notwithstanding one is more intelligent than the other, have no beginning; they existed before, they shall have no end, they shall exist after, for they are gnolaum, or eternal" (Abraham 3:18).

Now, at first it might seem unfair that the Lord called some spirits "more intelligent" than others. But remember our lesson on stars. Each star is different: each has different attributes, each is at a different stage in its development, and each has a different mission. Likewise, each child of God is different: we each have different attributes or talents, we each are at a different stage in our eternal development, and we each have a different mission on this earth. Because we are God's children, He perfectly knows us and what gifts and talents we brought with us to this earth. He has placed us on this earth at this time and in our current situation so that we can best grow, develop, and fulfill our mission here on the earth. Just like the sun, each of you has the perfect attributes and qualities you need to fill the measure of your creation.

If we continue to read in Abraham, the Lord explains, "These two facts do exist, that there are two spirits, one being more intelligent than the other; there shall be another more intelligent than they; I am the Lord thy God, I am more intelligent than they all" (Abraham 3:19).

By combining these two verses, we learn some important truths about ourselves. First, we learn that we are not all the same. There will always be someone more intelligent or more gifted in something than you are; likewise, you will be more intelligent or gifted with some attribute than someone else is.

But we also learn that we are eternal. While all the stars you see in the sky will eventually die, you will live forever. That means you have an infinite amount of time to change and to grow. You are not stagnant. You are a spirit son or daughter of God, and, as such, you have inherited the potential to become like Him. And because He is the most intelligent of all, each of us can grow in intelligence and ability to become like Him and eventually become perfect, as He is.

Perfection won't happen in this life, but you will carry with you into the next life the growth and development you obtain in this life, and these will give you that much more advantage in the life to come as you continue in your quest to become like our Father in Heaven (see Doctrine and Covenants 130:19).

In this day of Facebook, Snapchat, and Twitter—pick your favorite social media app—it is easy to get caught in the trap of comparing your life to the lives of others and to feel that your life is somehow lacking. When we are caught up in the race to perfection, setbacks, challenges, trials, and failures can seem overwhelming. Remember the lesson on stars. We are not all the same. We are not all meant to be the brightest star, the largest star, or the hottest star. In fact, we may not even be meant to be a star, and if we keep comparing ourselves against something that we are not, we will never find true happiness in this life. We will never become the person our Heavenly Father wants us to become.

In my research, I study objects called brown dwarfs. The

scientific community often refers to these objects as "failed stars" because they form like a star out of a cloud of gas and dust but don't have enough mass to ignite hydrogen fusion in their cores. Thus, they never become stars.

I hate the label "failed stars" because these objects were never meant to be stars! They were created to be brown dwarfs. And they are amazing!

When a brown dwarf first forms, it is relatively hot, but without an internal energy source, it slowly cools over time. Some of the younger and more massive brown dwarfs are as hot as the coldest stars at 3,500 degrees kelvin, while some of the older and less massive brown dwarfs have temperatures near 200 degrees kelvin. That is colder than the earth!

As these objects cool, clouds form in their atmospheres, similar to the cloud formation we see on Earth or on Jupiter. With their cloud structures, brown dwarfs look a lot more like planets than stars.

Brown dwarfs provide valuable knowledge for scientists who want to understand the atmospheres of gas giant planets that are orbiting other stars. You see, it is almost impossible to directly image a gas giant planet around its parent star. The star is so much brighter than the planet that we cannot directly detect light from the planet with our current technology. But since a brown dwarf is isolated in space and is not in orbit around another star, it can easily be studied to determine the properties of its atmosphere and cloud structure. Because the temperatures of brown dwarfs are similar to what we find for the gas giant planets, we can apply our knowledge of brown dwarf atmospheres to make assumptions of what the atmospheres of these extrasolar planets must be like.

Thus, brown dwarfs provide astronomers with essential knowledge that could be obtained in no other way. They perfectly fill the measure of their creation and are not failed stars. If anything, they are overachieving planets.

You Are a Child of God

The next time you doubt your self-worth or feel you are lacking as you compare yourself to others, remember that you are a child of God. You are His creation, and you are perfect in who you are meant to be. Reach out to Him, and He will help you discover the gifts and talents He has given you and the mission He has for you in this life. None of us are failures.

Like Abraham, Moses also had the privilege to talk with God face-to-face and to be shown the earth and all the inhabitants of the earth. I want to highlight some of the scriptures in Moses 1 as we conclude today.

In verses 3 and 4, God instructs Moses, "Behold, I am the Lord God Almighty, and Endless is my name; for I am without beginning of days or end of years; and is not this endless? And, behold, thou art my son; wherefore look, and I will show thee the workmanship of mine hands."

Remember, you are a son or a daughter of God. Let that knowledge inspire you to take the time each day to seek His guidance in your life. If you will just look and just ask, He will reveal truths unto you—truths you need to know.

In verse 6 God instructs Moses, "And I have a work for thee, Moses, my son." Can each of you hear God's voice speaking to you in your heart, telling you that you are His son or His daughter and that He has a work for you?

God continues: "And thou art in the similitude of mine Only Begotten; and mine Only Begotten is and shall be the Savior, for he is full of grace and truth" (Moses 1:6). God created you. He created you in His likeness and in His image, and He provided a Savior for you because He wants you to return to Him. He is doing all within His power to make it possible for you to gain exaltation. You just have to choose His path and endure to the end.

God concludes by telling Moses, "But there is no God beside me, and all things are present with me, for I know them all" (Moses 1:6). God knows you! He knows all His children. He knows your strengths, and He knows your weaknesses. He knows precisely what you need to do in this life to return to Him, to partake of His glory, and to become like Him. Let that knowledge inspire you to put your full trust in Him, and commit now to follow the promptings that He sends you.

Knowing that he was a son of God inspired Moses and gave him the strength he needed to withstand Satan. When he knew his divine nature, Moses made the commitment to serve God, to worship Him only, and to continually call upon the name of God (see Moses 1:13, 17–18). Likewise, each of us can take strength in knowing that we are children of God and are of infinite worth. That knowledge can see us through our most difficult challenges and struggles, especially if it inspires us to continually call upon God for help and guidance.

Remember to Look Up

When you are most weighed down with anger or doubt, if you can remember to look up and behold God's vast creations, you will be reminded of your eternal nature and that your current challenge or struggle is just a small moment in the time frame of eternity.

Remember that after the Lord showed Moses this incredible vision of the earth and taught him about worlds without number and that there was no end to His works, the Lord explained to Moses the purpose of this earth: "For behold, this is my work and my glory—to bring to pass the immortality and eternal life of man" (Moses 1:39).

Among all of our Father in Heaven's vast creations, you are the focus of His work and His glory. While earths will come and go and stars will live and die, you are eternal. Your exaltation is the reason for the creation of everything you see around you.

Remember that our Father in Heaven knows you and loves you. You are His child and "the workmanship of [His] hands" (Moses 1:4), and He wants nothing more than for you to return to Him and become like Him someday.

Never forget to look up. He is there, and He is waiting for you, and He will help you find your place in this universe.